CREATURE of WORSHIP

"God is a Spirit: and they that worship Him must worship Him in spirit and in truth."

John 4:24

Bishop Peter L. Coetzee (D.Div.)

KINGDOM BOOKS

Your kingdom come, your will be done

National Library Board, Singapore Cataloguing-in-Publication Data

Name(s): Coetzee, Peter L.
Title: Creature of worship / Bishop Peter L. Coetzee (D.Div.)
Description: Singapore: Kingdom Books, an imprint of Creative
    Juices Books [2016]
Identifier(s): OCN 959940816 | ISBN 978-981-09-8541-7
    (paperback)
Subject(s): LCSH: God (Christianity)--Worship and love. |
    Worship. | Christianity.
Classification: DDC 248.3--dc23

"I have known Bishop Dr Peter Coetzee for 35 years. To my knowledge, this book has been forming in his spirit long before then, and I view the book as a culmination of God's revelation to the man of God on this important subject. He is a true example of a creature of worship! To watch him worship stimulates one to ascend the hill of the Lord! In appreciation of this book, I have invited him to come over to our church in Pietermaritzburg, to preach and teach the message of the book to God's people. It is my belief that this message will bring the Church back to the epicenter of true worship!

"I pray for God's richest blessings upon *Creature of Worship* and for a glorious spiritual awakening in the lives of all who read it! I want to recommend this book without reservation to all Pastors, Leaders, Bible Scholars, and Christian believers everywhere! Your spiritual life will never be the same again!"

Bishop John Van Niekerk
Senior Pastor*: City Harvest Church*
Leader*: End-Time Harvesters*
Pietermaritzburg, South Africa

"Creature of Worship is a humble, yet powerful appeal to answer the call of Heaven—that we would walk in holiness and obedience. Dr Coetzee's inspired revelation parallels the Prophet Ezekiel's divine vision of worship. This is a must-read, not just for Pastors and Worship Leaders, but for anyone who wants to experience the kind of divine fellowship man first experienced before the fall."

Pastor David Ritter: Worship Pastor
Sonrise Community Church
Santee, California, USA

"Creature of Worship offers a glorious eye-opening experience on the subject of "True Worship". This Holy Spirit inspired presentation brings divine illumination to a key area in the life of the believer. Not only does it give a clear understanding of the subject, it also directly challenges the reader to respond to this revelation of true worship.

"I trust that each and every believer on the face of the earth will get to read this book and experience the significant life-changing transformation it offers! I pray that God will truly bless the writer of this significant book in its national and international distribution."

Bishop Edward P Clark: Moderator/Presiding Bishop
The Christian Assemblies Church International
Cape Town, South Africa

"Dr Coetzee's book should be welcomed by all believers who want to know more about worship. Pastors in general and Worship Leaders in particular should find the insights in the book very inspirational. The success in the contemporary church owes a great deal to excellence in worship, which makes Dr Coetzee's contribution an idea whose time has come."

Pastor Trevor Herbert
Regional Chairman, *Western Cape*
Executive member*: Apostolic Faith Mission of South Africa*

"This book is really long overdue, but it has come at the appropriate time in which we live. With *Creature of Worship*, we have experienced God in a totally different way, and our souls have been blessed and fed in a very special way. Our whole approach to worship has undergone a radical change. We pray that millions more will gain the same experience!

"Sharing its contents recently with some women at our church resulted in two souls coming to Christ in repentance. We do not think anyone who has read this book will remain the same. Understanding its contents necessitates a paradigm shift in the area of worship.

"Every Christian needs to read this book! It will change your life forever! May God richly bless this book and its author!"

Pastors Isaac and Mary-Jane Gordon: Senior Pastors
Potters House Pentecostal Ministries
Kraaifontein, South Africa

"*Creature of Worship* is not just another book on worship, but also an in-depth study which gives us a deeper insight and understanding of what 'True Worship' is all about. It speaks to the heart and soul of mankind, taking us to a higher level of 'True Worship'".

Pastor Dennis Francis (Licentiate in Theology)
Co-Founder & Vice-Chairman:
Redeemed Pentecostal Assemblies
Presenter *on the biggest Community Gospel Radio Station in Cape Town, South Africa:*
Radio Tygerberg-104FM STEREO

"This amazing book truly is inspiring, thought-provoking, and easy to read and understand. Dr Coetzee, who is also my Spiritual Father, has always been a man of high spiritual integrity, and this attribute comes through strongly in this book.

"How awesome! Man, the crown of God's creation, perfectly fitted God's requirements as His Creature of Worship! All the important aspects regarding true worship are clearly explained in this book. I truly see this book as an important study guide and source of education and information for any serious theological student seeking truth on this very important subject. The author's explanations and interpretation of the subject are deep and intensive.

"This book raises the curtain on how worship should be conducted in order to experience God's continuous holy presence. This surely is a long-awaited revelation! I hope that readers around the world will experience the same joy, edification and spiritual uplifting that I did when I read this book!"

Bishop Dr Frederick AG Thys: Senior Pastor
Victory Lighthouse International Ministries
New Commandment Pastoral Seminary &
Academy of Theological Studies
Westbank, Cape Town, South Africa

Contents

Dedication

Throughout our lives, God divinely and supernaturally orchestrates our paths so that we meet and connect with special persons destined to impact us. I therefore want to dedicate this book to these very special people and give recognition to those who, over many years, have positively touched my life and ministry. They have invested their lives and gifts into the ministry which I now cherish, honour and enjoy.

Firstly to my dad, the late Reverend Gert Marthinus Coetzee, and my mom, the late Maria Dorothea Coetzee, both of whom I love very dearly. As the youngest of ten children, I was privileged to grow up in a Christian home under their leadership and guidance. It was my dad who was my pastor and mentor; he taught me all I needed to know about true worship. He preached God's Word with passion, conviction, boldness and sincerity. It was he who, while I was still in my teens, prophesied that God's Hand was upon my life and that I would one day become a Servant of Almighty God.

Then, especially to my mom, who really was the prayer warrior in our home. She prayed continuously for her children through the day and many times all through the night too. As a result of those faithful and sincere prayers, all of their children are saved and some have already joined them in heaven.

Today I am what I am because I was blessed to have had God-fearing parents who lived exemplary, holy lives and who were our role models and examples of real and true worshippers.

I also need to acknowledge the powerful roles played by a few other special men of God, one of whom was the late Bishop JJC Titus of the Western Cape District—Pastor, Apostle, and National Leader of the Christian Assemblies. Here was a humble Servant of God who operated strictly under the Leadership of the Holy Spirit. Much of my spiritual growth and training as a leader took place under his able leadership.

Special thanks are due also to the late Bishop Michael Meyer, the founder of the Redeemed Pentecostal Assemblies in South Africa. He was my dear friend, father, mentor, and ministry associate and colleague. Together, we completed many fruitful years of successful ministry throughout South Africa. I sincerely appreciate the times we spent together, preaching the Gospel of deliverance over many years.

Also to the late Frank Weber, a powerful man of God, a Pioneer Evangelist, a precious humble Servant of God, and a true worshipper. For many years, he faithfully served the Church throughout South Africa, without much recognition and without appropriate accolade or remuneration; but he remained faithful to God's call right to the very end of his life. I am very sure and certain that his sacrificial service in God's divine Kingdom on earth has been appropriately recognized, acknowledged and rewarded in heaven.

These special people were instrumental in the formative years of my ministry, and much of what I know today—as a man of God, a true worshipper, and a leader in the Kingdom of God—was transferred by example into my life by these sincere and anointed men and woman of God. I honour the memory of these true worshippers and faithful soldiers of the Gospel of Christ.

Finally, I also want to dedicate this book to the memory of the late Reverend Dr Samuel G Hines of Washington DC in the USA. My life and ministry were deeply impacted, touched and radically changed by the dynamic ministry of this extraordinary man of God, with whom I was privileged to make acquaintance in 1979. I truly honour his memory, and I know that the impact his ministry had on the lives of countless thousands around the world is still bearing fruit in the Kingdom of God.

The glorious ministries of all these men of God—who were my Spiritual fathers, mentors and role models—will continue into eternity through my ministry and the ministries of many other Servants of God whose lives they also impacted.

Last, but not least, I need to take time and dedicate this book to my dear and precious wife Sidonia, without whose support the writing of this book would not have been possible. Also to our only child and daughter Lavinia and our son-in-law Rich, whom we have adopted as our own—both involved in worship ministry in Canada—and to our two beautiful and very special granddaughters Evangeline and Gabrielle. These precious people are so very dear to me. I really love, respect and appreciate them very, very much. Thanks for your love, support and encouragement over the years, especially during the time of writing this book. Your prayers and continuous support are greatly appreciated.

Then, finally, I dedicate this book to the memory of our late daughter Evangeline, who 43 years ago left us for heaven after only one day on earth. She is right now in God's Holy presence, worshipping Him in spirit and in truth. We cherish her dear and precious memory forever.

GOD RICHLY BLESS YOU ALL! I LOVE YOU!

Acknowledgments

I sincerely wish to thank each and every one who has supported me in this amazing project. Thank you for your prayers, encouragement and interest in this book.

Thanks especially to my dear wife Sidonia, our daughter Lavinia, her husband Rich, and our grandchildren Evangeline and Gabrielle for their prayers, unfailing love and constant support.

Thanks also to our proof readers, Pastor Dennis Francis, Marlene Coetzee-George, Zelda Davids, and Deone Wardle.

My thanks go also to Biblayah, our Ladies' Dance Ministry, and to our photographer, Radcliffe Roelse of Roelse Events, for the worship pictures in this book.

Special thanks, too, to the pastors and servants of God for their valued comments and their endorsements of this book.

Thanks once again. God bless you all abundantly!

Foreword

We live in an age when confusion and deception are rampant in the Church. Many preachers come to the body of Christ with various visions and revelations that lead to division, strife, competition and hatred. However, God is true to His Word! He will raise up godly men and women with clean hearts, spirits and motives; men and women of God who will clearly hear the voice of the Holy Spirit speaking to the Church; who will speak words of encouragement that will uplift believers, restore unity among us, and eventually bring us back to the heartbeat of Almighty God. That is true worship of God!

My dear friend and spiritual father, Dr Coetzee, brings with his message, *Creature of Worship*, a fresh and profound word to the Church for this hour!

He delineates and dissects the Word in such a profound manner that it will reach right into the heart of every believer. I firmly believe that, when the fragrance of true worship goes up to the Father, the blessings of God will come down! True worship to Almighty God needs to be restored in our personal lives, in our quiet times, in our homes, in our workplaces, and in our churches. God will restore wealth and prosperity in the Church and in our personal lives when we become true worshippers!

I therefore congratulate my dear friend on his encouraging word for this age. Thanks for being sensitive to the voice of the Holy Spirit! May this book ignite a fresh hunger for true worship in the hearts of all who read it! In our church, Living Waters International, we believe in Ephesians 3:20, which says that God can do super abundantly, far over, above and beyond what we can dream, think, imagine, pray and ask, because of His power at work in us!

I speak this word over this book and over Dr Coetzee's ministry: that it will reach every church and believer, to the four corners of the Earth! I pray that every believer will receive the full picture of this revelation and word for our season!

May God richly bless you!

Bishop Dr Raymond PE Olckers
Founder and Senior Pastor
Living Waters Worship Centre International
Belhar, Cape Town, South Africa

Introduction

From the very first verse in the book of Genesis to the very last verse in the book of Revelation, the Bible—God's Holy Word—addresses but one subject consisting of just one word. That word is "Worship".

Worship is and has always through the ages been the core imperative in God's communication and interaction with the human race. Worship is the very essence of God's eternal existence. God wants us to worship Him alone. He demands that we worship Him alone. He and He alone ought to be worshipped.

Creature of Worship unveils and addresses this very eminent subject of worshipping Almighty GOD our Father and Creator; it deals with the issue of true worship as declared and prescribed by our Lord Jesus Christ to the Samaritan woman at Jacob's well.

Our Lord Jesus tells us in *John 4:23-24* that "God is a Spirit" and that He is seeking people willing to "worship Him in spirit and in truth." The way I understand the precedent Jesus set in these verses is that this is the only kind of worship acceptable to Him: true, holy worship, "in spirit and in truth".

Today, all around the world, billions of people in every nation are engaged in some form of worship. Many of them do not even understand why they are worshipping their gods. Our inherent desire for worship has been with us since the dawn of creation. We have been created with a natural desire to worship. People *want* to worship. They *have* to worship. They will worship anything and anyone at any time, even if they do not fully understand the very purpose for which they were created.

God expects us to worship Him and Him alone, and to do so in spirit and in truth. In this book, I have tried to address the importance of the purpose for which we were created. God is a jealous God. He is a no-nonsense God. He created us for Himself, and He expects from us nothing less than total allegiance and unquestioning loyalty.

For too long we have been serving other gods. Regrettably, we have pledged our allegiance and loyalty to so many other gods and deities, to the exclusion of our Creator-God, who desires that we return to worshipping Him only. He desires to be to us the all-sufficient, sole object of worship and the sole source of our daily existence and supply.

I recognize and acknowledge that many thousands of writers, teachers and scholars have over the centuries debated on this important subject and written numerous books about it. Why, then, another book on worship? Firstly, this book was written to complement and enhance those other well-documented volumes. Secondly, it was written as a result of a divine revelation intended to be shared for the edification of the body of Christ around the world.

INTRODUCTION

Creature of Worship was birthed out of a divine encounter that I had with God the Holy Spirit some years ago. This encounter brought about a total transformation in my spiritual life and completely revolutionized my personal understanding of what it meant to worship Almighty God. Out of this divine encounter came a revelation of something so fantastic that I was constrained by the Holy Spirit to write and share it with the rest of God's people everywhere.

Much of what I share in these pages, you may possibly already know. But some truths will be new to you, just as they were brand-new revelations to me. I do hope the impression is not inadvertently created that I am an expert in this field and that I know more than anyone else about this important subject. Well, this is not the case. However, I can with confidence affirm, as Paul the Apostle did when he boldly told the church in Corinth, "I have received of the Lord that which also I delivered unto you..." (*1 Corinthians 11:23a*).

For I am certain that I too have heard from God. I know I have had an encounter with God the Holy Spirit and I have received revelations from the Lord regarding this key and crucial subject of worship; and, in humble obedience to the instructions of my Master, I have written this book. It is my prayer that you will understand and accept the contents of this book in that same spirit in which it was written.

I pray that you will be gloriously enriched, spiritually edified, and abundantly blessed, as you read this Holy Spirit-inspired book. I trust that this book will stir up a hunger in the heart of someone somewhere for God's Holy Presence, for His Divine Glory, and for His precious anointing which accompanies true, genuine worship. May you and I be truly transformed into God's holy "Creatures of Worship"!

Worship in Spirit and in Truth

Our Lord Jesus, in His conversation with the Samaritan woman at Jacob's well, made this important statement:

> But the hour cometh, and now is, when the true worshippers shall worship the Father in spirit and in truth: for the Father seeketh such to worship Him.
>
> God is a Spirit: and they that worship Him **must** worship Him in spirit and in truth.
>
> *John 4:23-24*

Please note that our Lord used the word "must" here—which means that it is absolutely imperative, crucial, necessary and essential, and that God expects nothing less than this utmost requirement when it comes to worshipping Him. *We must worship Him in spirit and in truth.*

What our Lord also meant was that, since the beginning of time, God has been searching for a certain kind of people. A people willing to become true worshippers of Him alone, worshipping Him in spirit and in truth. This is the only kind of worship that is acceptable, suitable and tolerable to Him. This search began the day He created man in His own image and likeness, as recorded in the book of Genesis chapter 1.

INTRODUCTION

Man was created by God for the purpose of enjoying a blessed, successful and fruitful life, and for the specific purpose of respecting, honouring and worshipping Almighty God the Creator, in spirit and in truth—thus establishing and obtaining dominion and control over everything God had created on the Earth.

We know what happened to the first created man and the wife God created for him, namely Adam and Eve. They started off together as true worshippers, worshipping God in spirit and in truth, communing and communicating with Him 24/7. But then unfortunately they failed because of their disobedience and half-hearted commitment and dedication to Creator-God.

Because they did exactly that which was forbidden by God, listening to the voice of the devil instead of the voice of their Creator, they were evicted from God's presence. It was a test of their obedience, commitment and dedication to the plan and order of Creator-God, but they missed it by not adhering to God's simple set of rules and instructions.

The key requirement and focus of God's search was and still is today for a people who will be totally committed, dedicated and sold out in absolute loyalty, allegiance and devotion to Him. A people who will worship Him in spirit and in truth; a people who will dedicate themselves to true worship of God and God alone at all times, in all circumstances and in all locations.

Today, all across the world, people of all nations are involved in some kind of worship. They worship many different gods and idols. There is a serious, desperate, inherent desire for worship. Humans are born with this strong, unquenchable desire for worship placed there by Almighty God, because within all of us resides our human spirit, which comes from God. We have been created as human beings with bodies of flesh, bones, arteries, veins, sinews and blood, within which our human spirit resides.

This human spirit makes us who we are. Without this human spirit inside of us, we would not be alive. The human spirit within us is what gives us life, vigour, identity, will and purpose. We are actually living spirits residing in bodies of flesh, bones, arteries, veins, sinews and blood; so that, when our spirit leaves its "home of flesh", our earthly existence immediately comes to an end.

In *Ecclesiastes 12:7* we read: "Then shall the dust return to the earth as it was; and the spirit shall return unto God who gave it." This truth is confirmed in *Genesis 3:19b*, where God declared: "For dust thou art, and unto dust shalt thou return."

Further confirmation regarding the concluding moments of our lives on earth comes from the descriptions of the crucifixion of our Lord Jesus and the stoning of Stephen, the first martyr in the Bible. *Luke 23:46* tells us that our Lord cried out with a loud voice, "Father, into Thy hands I commend my spirit"; and "having said thus, He gave up the ghost".

Then in *Acts 7:59* we read that, just before Stephen died, he cried out, "Lord Jesus, receive my spirit." So then, when our human spirit leaves our "bodies of flesh", it goes into God's care, into His hands. Then Almighty God alone has the sole right and prerogative to decide into which section of eternity our spirits will be sent.

Please also note that our spirits cannot die, because they come from God, who can never die. God lives in eternity forever and ever. He has always been, and He will forever be. Thus, when we die, our spirits will live forever, to spend eternity in one of two destinations: either in Heaven or Hell. *Revelation 20:15* declares, "And whosoever was not found written in the book of life was cast into the lake of fire." This lake of fire, also called hell, was created by God for the devil and his angels, and not for you and me (*Matthew 25:41*).

So, my friend, you and I have a choice as to where we will spend our eternity when we leave this life on earth. Will it be in heaven, in God's holy presence forever? Or will it be in hell, in the presence of Satan and his angels and demons forever? This extremely important choice about our eternal destination is yours and mine to make now.

Why not simply choose Jesus Christ as your Lord and Saviour? You will thus escape the everlasting horror and terror of a place of pain and never-ending tears! Call on Jesus now, ask for His forgiveness of all your sins and iniquities, and accept His immediate forgiveness, so that your name may be recorded in His Book of Life. You and I can escape an eternity in hell!

In *John 14:6*, Jesus declared, "I am the way, the truth, and the life: no man cometh unto the Father, but by me." Jesus Christ is the only way, the only truth, and the only life, the only One able to set us free from sin, iniquity and addictions. We need His forgiveness and deliverance and the Life only He can offer.

So, my friend, when Jesus speaks about us worshipping God "in spirit and in truth", He is referring to our human spirit needing to connect with truth. In other words, He requires the real, true, genuine you and me to connect to the genuine Truth, which is Him; because *He is the way, the truth, and the life*.

Jesus Is the Truth

Our Lord Jesus made an astounding statement in *John 8:32* when He declared, "And ye shall know the truth, and the truth shall make you free." So, if Jesus is the truth, then He is the one capable of setting us free. When we get to know Jesus Christ, we are actually acquainting ourselves with the Truth because *Jesus is the truth*.

Paul wrote in *Ephesians 4:21b*: "the truth is in Jesus". *Isaiah 65:16* refers to God as "the God of truth"; and the book of Deuteronomy describes our God in this manner:

He is the Rock, His work is perfect: for all His ways are judgment: a God of truth and without iniquity, just and right is He.

Deuteronomy 32:4

So, my friend, it is very clear, evident and unambiguous that God, through our Lord Jesus Christ, is the Truth and also the Author of truth. This fact is confirmed and affirmed in *Numbers 23:19*, which declares: "God is not a man, that He should lie; neither the son of man, that He should repent." So now please let me repeat:

- Jesus Christ, the Son of God, is the Way, and the Truth, and the Life.
- Since God the Father is the Truth, Jesus Christ His Son is the Truth.

Now, let us look again at our Lord's statement to the Samaritan woman at Jacob's well:

> But the hour cometh, **and now is**, when the true worshippers shall worship the Father in spirit and in truth: for the Father seeketh such to worship Him.
> God is a Spirit: and they that worship Him must worship Him in spirit and in truth.
>
> *John 4:23-24*

The words "and now is" show that Jesus was referring to worship *in the present tense*. The Father is today seeking people who will offer up to Him the only kind of worship that is acceptable, suitable and tolerable to Him. It is the kind of worship where we lose ourselves in His presence and forget about everything else; where we are totally consumed by God's Holy Presence; where all earthly things of human importance disappear into nothingness; where nothing else matters except pleasing the Father.

It is also the kind of worship that reaches out beyond the four walls of our sanctuaries and worship centres. It flows and overflows, out through the exit doors and into the street and alleyways of our towns and cities, where the needy, hungry, sick and destitute millions are waiting for help.

It is the kind of worship that cannot be contained within a room, a church building, an auditorium, or any structure erected by man. It has to break forth, break out, and break through all human limitations and restrictions.

It is the kind of worship that is constrained to go the extra mile with my brother, my sister, my friend, and my neighbour—even with my enemy! It drives me and moves me forward, upward and outward in all directions to fulfil my Master's assignment, to be what He has called me to be and to go where He sends me to go.

This is the kind of worship the Father is expecting from the true worshipper! Willing to become God's anointed Servant and the bearer of the Good News to those living with no hope for today and tomorrow! Worship in spirit and in truth means to become God's agents in and to a lost world! In fact, as true worshippers, our lifestyle must be one of worship each and every minute of every day, in everything we do!

Our Father must be and wants to be glorified in everything we say and do. The lives we live as true worshippers must reflect lives of worship in which our heavenly Father is glorified, honoured and respected in every move, act and conversation.

This is where our human spirit connects and joins with God's truth in Jesus Christ, and where we become His earthly ambassadors wherever we are. It is my prayer that our Father will help us to become part of His massive earthly team of true worshippers! I feel this is the only way that we, His people, can fulfil our earthly assignments as His disciples, charged with His commission to win the world for Christ.

Our Father is right now searching for you and me all across the globe! He is searching for true worshippers who will worship Him in spirit and in truth right here and now! Will we respond to His call? Will we answer His call today? Are we willing, just where we are across the globe, to join His massive army on earth and become His True Worshippers for the sake of winning souls for His divine Kingdom?

If you have said "Yes!" to His call, please make the following declaration with me now, and pray the prayer on the following page with me too.

Declaration

"I am a Creature of Worship, created by Almighty God to worship Him alone, in spirit and in truth."

Prayer

Heavenly Father, as I prepare to read this book, I ask your precious Holy Spirit to open my eyes that I may see, open my ears that I may hear, and open my mind that I may fully understand the revelation of your Word within the pages of this book.

Touch my life, change my life, and restore my life to that of a True Worshipper. I thank you, Lord. I believe it and I receive it. In the precious, holy and glorious Name of Jesus Christ our Saviour.

AMEN

CHAPTER ONE

In the Beginning, God!

Where it all began

The Bible, which constitutes the precious Word of God, contains the epic account of God's centuries-old search for true worshippers. It records His efforts to present the message of true worship in various ways through a multitude of different people—Prophets, Judges, Leaders, Apostles and Teachers. God's top priority has always been and still is His search for true and genuine worshippers.

The concept of worship in all of its glory was present right from the beginning. In fact, it goes even further back than the beginning—into eternity-past—when, in the very portals of heaven, God appointed a unique Seraphim named Lucifer to lead the hosts of heaven in worship before His Holy Throne.

This order of holy worship in heaven designed by God continued until this appointed Worship Leader, Lucifer, dared to defy God by wanting to be God and to become the object of worship in place of God. Scripture confirms that, as a result of his insolence and disrespect towards God, he was expelled from heaven. Friends, God will not share His glory with anyone, even with a Seraphim angel. He alone is God and He is passionate about His Honour and Glory!

When I think of the awesome greatness of God, the words of the world-famous hymn, "How Great Thou Art", come to mind. Written many years ago by Stuart K. Hine, the lyrics aptly depict God as the only one worthy of our worship:

> O Lord my God, when I in awesome wonder,
> Consider all the worlds Thy hands have made;
> I see the stars, I hear the rolling thunder,
> Thy power throughout the universe displayed—
> *Then sings my soul, my Saviour God, to Thee,*
> *How great Thou art! How great Thou art!*

In order for us to fully understand the purpose and importance of worship, it is necessary to go back to the very beginning of creation. God's Word declares, in *Genesis 1:1*, "In the beginning God created the heaven and the earth"... and everything else which followed His Creative Agenda.

Then, further on, we read in *Genesis 1:26-31* that God created man in His own image and gave him dominion over every living thing on the earth. God's clear instruction to man in verse 28 was: "Be fruitful and multiply, and replenish the earth, and subdue it."

God gave Adam a four-fold assignment: Prosperity, Multiplication, Replenishment and Dominion. Right at the beginning, we see God's divine plan and purpose for man. Not only should man and his wife be comfortable in their new home in the Garden, but it must also be well with him and his wife. Then, not only should it be well with them, but they should be prosperous. And, not only should they have enough, but they should have more than enough!

The fact that they should be prosperous and have more than enough was also not good enough, because the next step in man's management portfolio was the multiplication of his seed and of whatever they had access to. Whatever they lay their hands on would be blessed and multiply. And man was also given the task of replenishing the earth; he was given the responsibility of maintaining God's high standards of quality, excellence and adequacy. He had to ensure that there would always be more than enough for his family—and he had also to extend the family unit!

Then, as if all this were not enough, God finally conferred on Adam a fourth dimension of responsibility: He directed him to exercise dominion over *everything* He had created. Man was to be God's appointed representative on earth. He was to act as "God's Deputy", ruling the earth under God's ultimate Authority.

What an awesome job! What a glorious future awaited Adam and Eve as they started their matrimonial journey on the earth! They were totally in charge, under God's personal protection and authority. They were daily in constant and continuous fellowship with their Creator. There were no secrets, no hidden agendas, no fleshly desires, and no place for evil influences. Only truth, reality, genuine openness, and honesty with one another and with their Creator!

God the Creator was respected, honoured, feared and revered; and there was no hindrance to their relationship with their God. This holy, unblemished, 24/7 daily relationship with God was true worship in its purest form.

3

Each and every day they tasted, enjoyed and experienced the intimate presence and glory of God as they served and worshipped Him in the Garden. This was not only a privileged and marvellous experience, but it became their lifestyle—until they allowed themselves to be deceived by the evil one, Satan.

They were living in God's personal storehouse of inexhaustible abundance and, as earth's very first millionaires, they practically owned and managed the whole earth. And they did not even need a bank account! God supplied their every need, and they did not need to depend on any other source for their sustenance. God was their God, and He was their sole source of provision and existence.

What We Can Learn from Adam and Eve

What is it that God wants to reveal to us through the lives of the first two created humans? Four things. Firstly, God's perfection in all of creation. Everything created by God was perfect. God's Word declares, "And God saw everything that He had made, and, behold, it was very good" (*Genesis 1:31*).

We were all perfectly created by our Master Creator and, in the beginning, our first parents Adam and Eve were "True Worshippers" of God. We have, however, allowed ourselves to be deceived by the enemy. Now God requires that we return to our original status as true worshippers. We need to also take note that there was only one object of worship, namely GOD. He was at the heart of worship. Nothing else and no one else should interfere in this divine order.

Secondly, notice God's source of supply for us, if we are willing to return to the status of true worship, as it was in the Garden of Eden. There was no shortage or need in the Garden, because God's source of supply never became depleted. So, whatever we need is available in the Garden of True Worship. When our position and status as true worshippers get restored and re-established, the storehouse of God's provision will be at our disposal 24/7.

Thirdly, let us look at God's requirement for us to have dominion over our environment. God has placed Satan under our feet. Even though we have allowed ourselves to be deceived, the enemy has no right to rule over us and over our families. We had originally been given dominion by God to rule our environment. This dominion gets restored when we return to our original status as true worshippers. God wants to restore us to our rightful original status. The lifestyle of true worship expressed and exemplified by the first humans can be reclaimed as we come before God in humble consecration, confession and repentance.

Fourthly, notice the perfect fellowship and union between God and His created subjects. True worship was not difficult for them at all, because it was simply a normal and integral part of their daily lifestyle. Worshipping God 24/7 was neither difficult nor boring. It was an exciting and exhilarating walk with God every hour of every day. It was something they wanted to do continuously, because they loved fellowship with their Daddy, and they had a passion to worship Him.

Today, it is time for us to return to the Garden of our original status as true worshippers. We can once again enjoy the blessings of fruitfulness, prosperity, replenishment and dominion. This offer from God is still available. He has already made us the offer thousands of years ago. We can return to the Garden through our acknowledgment of God and our confession and repentance.

I believe God is waiting on us, His people, to return to Him. Let us return to the place of true worship. Let us be God's "Creatures of Worship". He is ready, willing and able to restore the broken lines of communication severed so very long ago. Come on friend, let's go. God is waiting!

God Demands Total Allegiance
(From the Beginning)

The following are foundational verses from the Law of Moses, given by God to His people. They establish, in no uncertain terms, God's prerogative as the one and only God to be worshipped:

Hear, O Israel: The Lord our God is one Lord:
And thou shalt love the Lord thy God with all thine heart, and with all thy soul, and with all thy might.

Deuteronomy 6:4-5

Thou shalt have none other gods before me.
Thou shalt not bow down thyself unto them, nor serve them: for I the Lord thy God am a jealous God...

Deuteronomy 5:7, 9a

Note also that God actually chose to use a murderer—Moses—to lead His people out of bondage. Moses had killed a man and was running away from the law when He encountered God along the way. One could actually say that, as he ran away from the law, he ran straight into God, the Giver and Author of THE LAW. God was about to teach Moses some of life's hard lessons. Even if the law cannot catch you, THE LAW (God's Law) will catch you!

Somehow, God will meet up with you and, when He does, He will take total hold of your life and your future. He will teach you His Law and transform you into His holy Servant. Hallelujah! He will show you and prove to you that HE ALONE IS GOD! God is passionate about His position as God. He demands your sole worship!

En route from Egypt to the Promised Land, Moses spent 40 days in seclusion with God on Mount Horeb, receiving God's Law for His people. While he was consumed in God's holy presence, the people were worshipping idols down in the valley. Returning from the mountain with the Law tablets, Moses saw their blatant idolatry in defiance of God's Law and, in frustration, smashed the tablets to smithereens against the rocks. As a result, he had to go up God's mountain for a second time to receive a fresh set of tablets.

But, even though Moses had smashed the first set of tablets, it did not mean that the Law on the second set was going to be different. God had not changed His mind about any of His Laws. So He gave Moses an identical set, exactly the same as the first.

God was and still is serious about our worship of Him alone. He alone is God, and He demands our sole worship. It is not too difficult to discover in Scripture the terribly destructive results of idol worship. All of the idolaters, the guilty ones, died in the desert. They allowed themselves to be deceived and robbed of God's eternal blessing and of their God-given inheritance of the Promised Land.

From the very beginning, God has been very serious about idol worship. God cannot and will not accept second place. He demands first place in our lives. He has no qualms about declaring Himself to Moses as *a jealous God!* My dear friend, God will not play second fiddle. He demands total allegiance. He demands that we worship Him alone, in spirit and in truth.

Right back at the beginning, God had major struggles with His people on the issue of worship. Throughout the journey of God's people to the Promised Land and even thereafter, God had great difficulty with their disobedience on the issue of true worship. Because of this, He instructed Moses to document and devote one whole chapter in the Pentateuch to blessings and curses. Obedience and worship are its main themes.

As we read Deuteronomy chapter 28, we begin to really grasp the importance of this subject of worship from God's perspective. All 68 verses in this chapter carry either a blessing or curse: blessings as a result of obedience and curses because of disobedience. God was drawing a line, establishing parameters of choice for His people.

He was placing the ball squarely in their court. They would be the ones to decide whether they would be blessed or cursed. Who were they going to obey? Who would they worship? Would they worship God? Or their own gods, their own desires, their lust and their flesh? The choice was theirs. The bottom line is that the obedient child of God will enjoy blessings, honour, safety, security and prosperity.

The true worshipper will reap all of the benefits recorded in Deuteronomy chapter 28. God has offered an indisputable, unequivocal guarantee of this. Even in the face of ridicule and opposition, the true worshipper will be protected and defended by God. Some of these true worshippers had to endure major trials, even to the point of endangering their lives, as their allegiance and loyalty to God were continuously tested to the limit.

Champions of worship like Daniel and his three friends, Shadrach, Meshach and Abednego, come to mind. These great heroes had no difficulty making up their minds about whom they would worship, even if in the process they would lose their lives. God in His faithfulness protected them each and every time, because of their steadfast boldness and trust in Him.

The Writing on the Wall

Daniel was a great, anointed man of God who was totally committed to the cause of serving Him 24/7 as a true worshipper. Here was someone who, from the beginning, made a clear and unequivocal decision to serve the God of his forefathers in spirit and in truth.

While in captivity, Daniel served successfully under King Nebuchadnezzar in Babylon. He was used by God as a prophet on several occasions to astound even the king's wise men. Through Daniel's ministry, this very same king was brought to his knees to acknowledge God Almighty as the only true God.

After Nebuchadnezzar came his son, King Belshazzar. Daniel chapter 5 records that one day Belshazzar invited all his high-profile friends to a party, in the course of which he commanded to be brought before him certain golden vessels, cups and chalices that his father Nebuchadnezzar had earlier taken from God's house. They had been sanctified for holy service to God, but he wanted to use them for his own pleasure. In so doing, he was challenging God's authority and defying His divine holiness.

Then we read in verse 5 that, at the climax of this drunken party, the king saw the fingers of a man's hand appearing before him and writing on the wall. Trembling in fearful shock, the king looked at the handwritten message, wanting to know its meaning; but no one was able to read the script or understand its meaning.

Then the king's wife mentioned to him Daniel's name, referring to the Prophet as a man "in whom is the spirit of the holy gods" (*Daniel 5:11*). Daniel was summoned to appear before the king, and he gave the king a message from Almighty God. The following were the words that the king had seen on the wall: "MENE, MENE, TEKEL, UPHARSIN."

Daniel translated God's message to the king as follows:

1. "MENE" – "God hath numbered thy kingdom, and finished it." (*verse 26*)
2. "TEKEL" – "Thou art weighed in the balances, and art found wanting." (*verse 27*)
3. "UPHARSIN" (which means "and Pharsin"; it can also be read as "Peres", the singular form of "Pharsin") – "Thy kingdom is divided, and given to the Medes and Persians." (*verse 28*)

One could actually translate the message into three simple words:

1. Numbered
2. Weighed
3. Divided

The Bible tells us in *Daniel 5:30* that the king was slain on that very same night. He died at the hands of his enemies.

Now, my friend, I have decided to pause at this portion of Scripture for a very good reason. If we look at this message from God, written on the wall by His very own hand; and, if we study its contents, we will find that this is actually a message to each and every person alive today. The message addresses three specific issues pertaining to our lives:

1. Our days on earth are *numbered*. Each one of us has been given a set number of days to live in this world. Here God is referring to the **Quantity** of our days.
2. The life we live daily is being *weighed* by God Himself. Here God is referring to the **Quality** of our lives.

3.   Thirdly, there is going to be a *division* taking place at the end of our days, which translates to the word ***Eternity***.

So we are looking at three very significant words with regard to our earthly lives:

1.   Quantity
2.   Quality
3.   Eternity

At the end of our days, you and I will stand before the judgment seat of Almighty God, and there will be a "division" that will take place. In *Matthew 25:31-46*, Jesus Himself gave a full explanation of this final process of division. He said that He would divide all the people, placing them either on His right or on His left.

Those on the right will be ushered into God's divine presence in heaven, where they will join those who have obeyed God's Word. But those on the left, who have been disobedient and stubbornly rejected God's Word, will be ushered into eternal damnation. This, my friend, is going to be the moment of truth for all mankind.

"Numbered, Weighed and Divided" then becomes a reality for each one of us. God has been fair to all of us by offering us quantity and quality; now comes eternity, from which there is no escape. For this reason, you and I, who are presently enjoying the quantity of days given to us, should ensure we are not weighed and found wanting by God. We need to live quality lives, serving and worshipping God in spirit and in truth—so that we will be granted God's grace of eternal life with Him when the day of division comes.

The Father of Many Nations

The life of Abraham is an epic story of faith. It is a chronicle of obedience and of the rewards in store for those who choose to follow and worship God unconditionally. It is a record of a true worshipper whom God eventually called His friend (*Isaiah 41:8; James 2:23*). Never before Abraham or after him has God called any other person His friend!

But, now, wait a minute. Here's the problem: how could God call this man His friend? Going back into the history of this "friend of God", we actually uncover a sordid life of idolatry. Wow! Would you believe that our holy God, who had declared Himself a jealous God, would show even the remotest interest in someone who openly worshipped idols?

What made such a Holy God turn to a relatively insignificant man living in a strange place called Ur of the Chaldees? It was a country of heathens. Idol worship was a lifestyle for those people.

As I ponder on this amazing development in Biblical history, I cannot but wonder what it was that moved God to go to this strange place in the middle of nowhere, to call this unknown man to become His friend. Surely God could have found a friend elsewhere?

Therefore God must have noticed something special, something of value in the life of this man Abram. I do believe that God must have noticed the man's attitude in his worship of those idols. He must have noticed spiritual integrity, seriousness, passion and dedication in Abram's commitment to his gods.

13

God might have thought, "If I can convince this guy to follow me and worship me with this kind of commitment, then I would have one true worshipper, through whom I can create nations of true worshippers."

So, what did God do? One day He simply appeared to Abram and instructed him to get up and leave his father's home, his family and his people. He had to leave his nation and move away from his country to follow God.

"Follow you? Where to, Lord?"

"Abram, just pack your bags and go. I'll show you later where you'll be going."

Humanly speaking, if this were you or me, we would certainly have some questions to ask God before even considering whether to obey Him. And the first question would probably be: "Who are you?"

And God answers, "Well, I am the God of the Universe. I am the One who created you and your family."

Then, I will ask, "What do you want from me?"

God answers, "I want you to pack your bags and leave your father's home, your family, your nation, and your country, and follow me."

I respond, "Follow you? Where to, Lord?"

Then God answers, "Well, once you have left, I will somehow, sometime, somewhere let you know where you are going."

"Lord, do you mean that I have to leave my home and everything dear and precious to me, and follow you to a place you do not even know?"

Then God says, "That's right. If you will obey me and follow me, you will be blessed beyond your wildest expectations!"

And my final answer will be, "Well, Lord, I don't know. Even though it sounds really good, the risk will be too enormous to even contemplate. And my other problem is... you see, Lord, I do not even know you! So, Lord, thanks, but no thanks, I think I'll pass."

This would probably have been the response of any right thinking, normal person, and it would certainly be an acceptable response; and to God it would certainly not have been an unreasonable, insulting or rude response.

But this was not Abram's response. The Bible declares that, without any question, hesitation, ridicule or inquiry, Abram simply obeyed God. Without one question, this 75-year-old idol worshipper immediately believed the words coming from the mouth of an unfamiliar God.

We read in *Genesis 12:4*, "So Abram departed, as the LORD had spoken unto him." This childlike faith of Abram, his trust in a God he did not even know or understand, touched the very heart of Almighty God.

Here we observe the character of a true worshipper: willing to leave everything near and dear to him and blindly obey God's instructions, even at the risk of failure. Abram totally surrendered his will to God's Will. His attitude can be summed up in this way: *"Whatever it takes and whatever the cost, I will follow God all the way, and I will worship Him in spirit and in truth."*

15

Then came the amazing blessing to Abram; God changed his name to Abraham and declared, "For a father of many nations have I made thee" (*Genesis 17:5*). The reward for a true worshipper, willing to pay the price of obedience to God at all cost, is a reward which will totally exceed our wildest expectations! I do believe this humble man moved the very heart of God, as He observed the passion of a true worshipper.

This man was willing to leave everything and go all the way with a God he had just met. Not only did he demonstrate faith, he also trusted God with his very life. Now, hear what God said about this devout and totally dedicated intercessor, when He sent His angels to pour judgment upon Sodom and Gomorrah. (God had by this time finally made up His mind to judge these two corrupt and sinful cities.) The respect that Almighty God revealed for one simple man is truly astounding and mind boggling. This is what He said:

> Shall I hide from Abraham that thing which I do;
> Seeing that Abraham shall surely become a great and mighty nation, and all the nations of the earth shall be blessed in him?
>
> *Genesis 18:17-18*

What an amazing person Abraham must have been, for God to even consider him and inform him first, before carrying out His plan to destroy those cities! God then once more reaffirmed His personal promise to Abraham, that he "shall surely become a great and mighty nation, and all the nations of the earth shall be blessed in him". How awesome! How astounding to hear such a statement from God Himself!

16

Our wonder over the relationship between Abraham and God increases even more when we read the very next verse—because God actually presented a personal testimonial or, as it were, a mini resume of this man. God declared of Abraham:

> **For I know him, that he will command his children and his household after him, and they shall keep the way of the LORD, to do justice and judgment; that the LORD may bring upon Abraham that which He hath spoken of him.**
>
> *Genesis 18:19*

Once again, my friends, I am absolutely dumbstruck at the impressive example of this true worshipper Abraham, the Friend of Almighty God and the Father of many nations. Here is the perfect example of what can be achieved by just one true worshipper who touches the heart of Almighty God and, in the process, creates world history. It seems that Almighty God will honour and show respect to the true worshipper who reaches the place of total surrender to His divine will and purpose.

Abraham's Legacy of Worship

Abraham's son Isaac arrived very late in his life. The promise that God had made to him, when he started out following Him, only came to fruition when he was 100 years old and his wife Sarah was 90. Only after 25 years of faithful and continuous worship did he begin to see God's promises slowly unfold with the birth of his son Isaac.

Then came the shock of his life—one that would test every fibre of his integrity. He had been waiting 25 years for something to happen in line with God's promise of an heir, and now God was telling him to kill the boy! But, because the man was a true worshipper, he believed and trusted God unreservedly and unconditionally.

In fact, while he was being tested to the very limit, he also put God to the test. According to *Hebrews 11:18-19*, he believed that, if he killed his son, God would bring the boy back to life—thereby placing the ball squarely in God's court! Well, we know what happened. God gave this humble but extraordinary man His official stamp of approval. Abraham was the very first human in history to become God's friend.

His son Isaac followed in his footsteps by fearing God and worshipping Him. God appeared to Isaac and repeated the promise He had made to his father Abraham. We read in *Genesis 26* how God promised to multiply his seed like the stars of heaven. He would give countries to them, and through them the nations of the earth would be blessed.

Isaac's son Jacob followed afterward; and, even though he faltered when he deceived his brother with the assistance of his mother, God forgave him and still blessed him because of the covenant He had made to his granddaddy Abraham.

God blessed Jacob with twelve sons, among whom Joseph was the one God chose to continue his great-grandfather's legacy. Joseph was ridiculed and hated by his brothers and sold as a slave to strangers in a foreign land. However, God divinely orchestrated amazing developments that brought this young man into Pharaoh's house.

Joseph was a true worshipper who feared God. He refused to yield to temptation but chose, even to his own detriment, to flee the spirit of adultery and stay pure in the sight of God. He obeyed and worshipped God in the midst of trials, temptations and opposition, and while enduring much pain, suffering and humiliation; and God eventually raised him up to become second-in-command in Egypt.

Then, finally, after many years of separation from his family, Joseph was vindicated when God used him to save the very brothers who had tried so hard to destroy him. His inspiring words moved even the hearts of those hardened men, when he declared in *Genesis 45:5*, "Now therefore be not grieved, nor angry with yourselves, that ye sold me hither: for God did send me before you to preserve life."

My dear friend, the true worshipper knows how to forgive wholeheartedly. The true worshipper accepts God's will, even if God is silent in the face of suffering and injustice. The true worshipper's main focus is to please God at all times. The true worshipper bears no grudges and carries no hatred in his heart against those who did him wrong.

The true worshipper is comfortable and satisfied in the knowledge that God is in charge and that He will take care of everything. The true worshipper is committed, dedicated and passionate in pleasing God and doing His will at all costs. In *John 15:14*, Jesus revealed to us God's requirement for friendship when He declared, "Ye are my friends if ye do whatsoever I command you."

Our Lord has made it abundantly clear that there is an uncompromising demand on anyone who would be a friend of God. This kind of special friendship demands from us total obedience to God's will and purpose. From the very beginning, God has been serious about true worship. He still is today. The Father is still searching for true worshippers, as our Lord Jesus declared to the Samaritan woman in John chapter 4. This has been an ongoing search over many centuries, and the search continues today. God is seriously and urgently seeking true worshippers. Will you respond?

CHAPTER TWO

Created for Worship

Why we were created

W hy did God create us? The Book of Revelation gives us the answer:

> Thou art worthy, O Lord, to receive glory and honour and power: for Thou hast created all things, and **for Thy pleasure they are and were created.**
>
> *Revelation 4:11*

In a nutshell, this verse tells us why we have been created. You and I were created for God's pleasure. You and I are here on earth as a result of God's grace and mercy. It therefore follows that our existence on earth should daily bring God pleasure. The way we live, the way we act, and the way we operate and interact with others should give God pleasure. The way we deal and interact with nature, our environment, and all the rest of creation should give God pleasure.

Revelation 4:11 further declares that three things are due to God: glory, honour and power. All humans are made in God's image. We carry His mark. God created us for His pleasure and divine purpose. Our earthly habitation is the place where He has placed us to live successful, happy and prosperous lives. Our lives and the things we do should bring glory, honour and power to His holy name. We have been created for worship. We are God's Creatures of Worship.

Our Desire for Worship

It is an undeniable fact that humans *want* to worship—whether we worship God, or idols of wood or stone, or any other earthly object, or even another human being. We want to worship because worship is an inherent part of our being.

People in countries and nations all over the world are somehow somewhere worshipping right now. Some nations are even worshipping several different gods, as they seek to find the only true and living God. This quest has been going on for many centuries now. But, until we accept Jesus Christ and bow our knees before Him, our lives will be meaningless. We will keep on searching until we find Him, who alone is worthy of our worship.

For thousands of years, billions of people have been deceived by Satan into believing they can find salvation, peace and satisfaction through different forms of idol worship. Because Satan knows how important worship is to us, he has conned billions by luring them away from the only true and living God.

In the previous chapter, we discovered just how serious God is about worship. He has zero tolerance when it comes to this important issue. Since He created us specifically for this purpose, He demands our total allegiance and loyalty. It is therefore our responsibility as worshippers to return to the living God, who alone deserves our true worship. Let us give Him glory and honour and power, as His creatures who worship Him in spirit and in truth.

Number One

We need to place God where He belongs, as Number One on our list of priorities. Worship should be our daily lifestyle, and not simply something we do on Sundays. Going to church to pray and to sing hymns, choruses and worship songs—this is not necessarily the worship He desires from us. He expects much more. People go to church for various reasons. Many do not necessarily go to worship God. It is important to understand that God desires true worship from the heart.

What is true worship? Well, it is more than simply attending church. It is more than what is mentioned above. True worship is honouring, respecting and fearing God. It is denying ourselves, taking up our cross, and following Jesus. It is focusing on what pleases God and doing what pleases Him 24/7. Jesus made this clear when He said, "And why call ye me, Lord, Lord, and do not the things which I say?" (*Luke 6:46*)

Then He went on to compare those who obey Him and honour His word to a wise man who builds his house on a rock. This house would withstand the storms and challenges of life (*Luke 6:47-48*). This is in contrast with those building on sand, who would not be able to survive the trials of life (*Luke 6:49*).

God expects true worship from us. He has created us for this very purpose, to do His will continually. As King David so aptly put it in *Psalm 34:1*, "I will bless the LORD at all times; His praise shall continually be in my mouth."

In *Psalm 34,* David revealed his 24/7 relationship with his God. Worship was a lifestyle to him: "at all times" and "continually" suggest a 24/7 worship relationship. I believe this to be one of the key reasons why God called David "a man after my own heart" (*Acts 13:22, NIV*).

What if today God could find men and women after His own heart around the world? Men and women willing to humble themselves and consecrate themselves to a 24/7 lifestyle? The world, the church, our communities, our homes, and our families would certainly not be the same!

God through His Holy Spirit would be able to change the hearts, minds and lives of countless millions around the globe. I believe we would begin to see a move of God, the like of which we have never seen before. You see, my friend, we have been created to be Creatures of Worship; so, when we return to God's order of worship, we will begin to bring back His glory into our midst.

I firmly believe with all my heart that God wants to return to our lives, our homes, our churches, and our nations in all of His glory, just like before. God's people need to set the standard of true worship. We need to set an example to the rest of the world as God's true worshippers.

"Be Ye Holy"

For too long, too much has been preached, declared, taught and published about the subject of worship, but without any real understanding of God's prerequisites for true worship. The very first prerequisite, declared in *Leviticus 19:2*, was: "Ye shall be holy: for I the LORD your God am holy."

True worship 24/7 will be unattainable without understanding the importance of holy living. God expects me to observe a holy lifestyle in which His holiness could be accommodated. For the believer, the blood-washed child of God, the Christian who declares Jesus Christ as Lord, this is not optional. It is obligatory. It is compulsory. It is a direct command from Almighty God: "Ye shall be holy." It is a requirement, a condition set by God Himself for those who dare to serve Him and belong to Him.

What does God mean when He calls His people to a life of holiness? What is it that we should or should not do? The answer to this question was already given earlier in this chapter, when we talked about Jesus asking, "And why call ye me, Lord, Lord, and do not the things which I say?" It is a simple fact: we ought to do what He says. Living a holy life begins by doing what God's Word says we ought to do.

The more we learn to obey God through His holy Word, the more we will be moving into a life of holiness. Doing what pleases Him is the key that unlocks the door to holiness. Jesus knew this was the key; it had been proven and tested by Him throughout His life on earth. To Him, this was of utmost importance: simple obedience to His Father without question, and at all times doing only what pleases Him. The success of His mission on earth was based on this very important key. Over and over again, He stressed His total commitment to doing only the will of His Father. Nothing more, nothing less.

What a marvellous example we see from the Master Himself! Even when the time came for Him to complete the final chapter of His life on earth, He was still totally dependent on and committed to the will of His Father. He prayed, "Father, if Thou be willing, remove this cup from me; nevertheless not my will, but Thine, be done." (*Luke 22:42*)

My dear friend, the true worshipper will follow this glorious example of the Master Worshipper: total dedication and commitment to doing the will of the Father 24/7, even if it means the end of one's existence on earth! This, my friend, is the heart of true worship for real! Oh, how God is today still seeking people who are willing to totally surrender themselves to Him!

A Holy Nation for the Lord

From the beginning of creation, God has desired a people for Himself: a Holy Nation that will be totally consecrated for service to Him alone. God has been looking for a nation that will be His very own for all eternity, because we have certainly been created to live forever.

Unfortunately, this plan fell through when man dismally failed his initial test. We succumbed the very first time we were tempted. But God has not given up on us yet. He is still interested in establishing a Holy Nation for Himself. Through His prophet Zechariah, God declared that He would bring His people back to the land He had given them. He promised, "And they shall be my people, and I will be their God in truth and in righteousness." (*Zechariah 8:8b*)

God is still interested in having a people for Himself. He has asserted, "I was jealous for Zion with great jealousy... I am returned unto Zion, and will dwell in the midst of Jerusalem" (*Zechariah 8:2-3a*). God is a God of truth and righteousness. He seeks a nation of truth and righteousness for Himself. *Proverbs 14:34* corroborates this, when it declares that "Righteousness exalteth a nation; but sin is a reproach to any people." So too the prophet Isaiah, when he cried out, "Open ye the gates, that the righteous nation which keepeth the truth may enter in." (*Isaiah 26:2*)

God's Qualifications for a Holy Nation

Through His prophet Zechariah, God has set down His qualifications for a holy nation:

> These are the things that ye shall do; Speak ye every man the truth to his neighbour; execute the judgment of truth and peace in your gates:
>
> And let none of you imagine evil in your hearts against his neighbour; and love no false oath: for all these are things that I hate, saith the Lord.
>
> *Zechariah 8:16-17*

Those who desire to be a part of this international universal "Holy Nation" should:

1. Speak the truth to one another;
2. Execute judgments of truth and peace;
3. Not imagine evil in their hearts against one another;
4. Not love false oaths; in other words, live righteously and oppose corruption on any level and at all times.

27

In verse 17, God said, "these are things that I hate." Friend, God hates lies, deceit and cheating. We need, firstly and urgently, to return to the Biblical virtues of truth and honesty. Secondly, truth and peace, which have lately become seemingly rare commodities, need to return to our lives, homes and communities. Thirdly, we ought not to imagine evil in our hearts against one another; and we should not wish or pronounce evil on other people either.

Fourthly, we need to withstand and rebuke the evil of corruption and unrighteousness wherever it shows itself in every area of our lives today. As the prophet Isaiah lamented, "Judgment is turned away backward, and justice standeth afar off: for truth is fallen in the street, and equity cannot enter!" (*Isaiah 59:14*) This is as true today as in Isaiah's day; we need stand up for righteousness at all times.

We, as God's holy nation, should set the standard in our communities. The things that God hates should also be hated by His people. Truth, honesty, peace and righteousness should be the order upon which we build our lives, our homes, our churches, our communities, and our nations. As the Apostle Peter reminded us in *1 Peter 2:9*, we are indeed a chosen generation, a holy nation and a people of His own, and we should show forth the praises of Him who has called us out of darkness into His marvellous light.

Psalms 33:12 reiterates this; it declares, "Blessed is the nation whose God is the LORD; and the people whom He hath chosen for His own inheritance." Please note the words: ***chosen for His own inheritance***.

Friend, God has redeemed us from every nation on earth and united us as one people: His people, His holy Nation. We now belong to Him. We are His property, a righteous and blessed nation, a prosperous nation. God's Holy Nation! Let us today rededicate ourselves, our families, our communities and our nations to God. Let us turn to Him in repentance, in truth, in righteousness, in holiness. Hallelujah!

As the people of God, whom God has united into one Holy Nation for Himself, our prerequisite and priority should be to live a life of holiness and submission to our Master, Lord and King. Let us once again consecrate our gifts, our talents and our abilities to Him.

Let us also reaffirm our status in Him today. We are members of His divine Kingdom on earth. As such, we are called to live a dedicated life, in which true worship of God 24/7 is the main purpose of our daily existence. If ever there was a time when worshippers should step up to the plate of honesty, reality and repentance, and be transformed into God's true worshippers, that time is now!

We have had enough conferences, conventions, seminars and workshops on worship to last us more than a lifetime. These dynamic gatherings have been hosted and officiated by some of the world's most renowned speakers, pastors, teachers, apostles and prophets. Our lives have been challenged, touched, stirred, moved and shaken; but, alas, we have not as yet been changed. We have not truly and fully comprehended the message and its real implications for our lives. We may have managed to ingest the word, but we have not thus far adequately digested its contents.

Hearing, Doing, Being

Earlier in this chapter, I showed how Jesus contrasted hearers of the Word with doers of the Word. I do believe that God in His infinite wisdom has added another dimension to this divine equation: to be a Being of the Word. First we hear, then we do, then we become. I become a being, a creature, His creature, willing to be what He created me to be. I become His Creature of Worship.

In our day, we have more than enough hearers who daily hear God's Word preached and taught around the globe. I tend to think we also have a good percentage of doers of the Word around the world. However, there still seems to be certain things holding us back from becoming and being what God had created us to be.

Becoming and being like Christ should indeed be the ultimate goal for us as God's people. We certainly understand that this is a lifelong process. To be like Jesus should therefore be the main priority on our agenda. We are exhorted in several Scriptures to follow after Christ's example. Jesus declared, "If any man serve me, let him follow me... if any man serve me, him will my Father honour." (*John 12:26*)

Jesus is very clear about the reward for those who are willing to serve and follow Him. He says they will be honoured by His Father. To be honoured by God is to be blessed with something all the riches on earth can never buy. We find ourselves enjoying the favour of God, the Creator of the universe!

Then we read in *Philippians 2:5*, "Let this mind be in you, which was also in Christ Jesus." Here we are exhorted to have the mind of Christ, for if we can have the mind of Christ, then our lives will surely follow His example of honouring our heavenly Father in true worship.

We are also promised, in *1 John 3:2b*, that "when He shall appear, we shall be like Him; for we shall see Him as He is." This encourages us to press on, so that our efforts to become like Christ will finally be rewarded. The promise is that we shall then be like Him. It will be the culmination of our long earthly struggle, since our eviction from the Garden of Eden; all our sufferings will conclude in a glorious fashion, when we shall be changed to finally be like Jesus.

The Temple of the Holy Spirit

God has prepared for Himself a temple in which He wants to reside. In the Garden of Eden, He created a man's body and breathed His Spirit into that body, and the man became "a living soul". Since then, God's residence has been within each of us.

Paul the Apostle wrote thus to the church in Corinth: "Know ye not that your body is the temple of the Holy Spirit which is in you, which ye have of God, and ye are not your own?" (*1 Corinthians 6:19*) This body of ours is called the temple of the Holy Spirit. We do not belong to ourselves. Our bodies belong to God. He owns us because He created us. God holds full ownership of our bodies. He made them for one purpose, and that purpose is to worship Him alone.

Then, in *1 Corinthians 3:17*, we find this shocking warning: "If any man defile the temple of God, him shall God destroy; for the temple of God is holy, which temple ye are." God expects us to keep this temple—this body of ours—holy, or else He will destroy us. Now, my friend, that is serious! He is willing to destroy our bodies should they be defiled because of wilful sin, iniquity or idol worship!

What God is actually saying, is that our bodies should be dedicated as holy temples of the Holy Spirit, ready and willing for 24/7 true worship of God alone! Friend, we need to be very careful what we put into our bodies; what we eat, drink or take into this holy vessel in diverse ways. Never before in history have we experienced such a massive increase in substance abuse and drug dependence.

Nations are defiling the temple of the Holy Spirit with devastating consequences. As I was preparing to write this book, I realized that what had happened in the Temple in Jerusalem, after Jesus died on the cross, was truly both miraculous and significant. *Matthew 27:51* tells us: "And, behold, the veil of the temple was rent in twain from the top to the bottom."

I do believe that, with the death of Jesus on the cross, God made a separation and drew a line between worship and true worship, worshipper and true worshipper. The curtain was torn from top to bottom. It was as if God was making a statement. He was breaking forth from out of the box, out from behind the curtain which separated the Holy of Holies, in order to come out and live among us, His people.

No longer would He be worshipped in one particular, designated location; but He would be worshipped everywhere, by every one of His creatures, as He wanted to be. Hallelujah! No longer would He be worshipped only in "the Holy place"; but we, His people, His Creatures of Worship, would now become His "Holy place". He has now truly become our Emmanuel, God with us! God among us! God in us! 24/7 true worship is now possible anywhere, at any time, by anyone.

The specific purpose for which we were created can now be accomplished without any restriction whatsoever. We now have no excuse for not worshipping God. Wow! What a wise and awesome God we serve! Not only is He wise and awesome but, my friend, He is very serious about worship! As you and I take responsibility to accomplish the purpose for which we were created, we will begin to experience the fullness of God's grace, mercy and blessings upon us and upon our families.

CHAPTER THREE

Experiencing True Worship

Worship before God's Throne

The important question that comes to mind as we ponder upon the subject of worship is, "What is true worship?" What does it mean? What is it really like? Well, we get a glimpse of it from the best scriptural demonstration and example of true worship we can find, in the book of Isaiah:

> In the year that king Uzziah died I saw also the LORD sitting upon a throne, high and lifted up, and His train filled the temple.
>
> *Isaiah 6:1*

In our attempt to fully understand the Prophet Isaiah's vision, it will be necessary to pause for a few moments and purposefully study the significance of the five astounding observations revealed in this verse of Scripture. Let us look at them and discover their amazing prophetic significance.

The five significant elements observed in *Isaiah 6:1*:

1. It was the year that King Uzziah died;
2. Isaiah saw the Lord;
3. Sitting on a throne;
4. High and lifted up; and
5. His train filled the temple.

Firstly, this glorious vision of true worship came in the year king Uzziah died. The earthly king who had occupied the earthly throne had to die before the heavenly King of kings sitting on His heavenly throne could be revealed and accommodated!

Visions of God's divine glory will only become visible to us when we are willing to allow the things reigning in our lives to die. The things occupying the throne of my heart, soul, life and existence have to be permanently removed. God is not the ruler of my life if another king sits on my throne. Those things which we have voluntarily crowned "king" over our lives for many years have to be forcibly removed from the throne of our hearts.

In the previous two chapters, we have come to realize that God wants our sole worship. He is a jealous God. He wants to occupy my throne—alone. When I submit my throne to God alone, then true worship becomes a reality. The other "kings" in my life have to die first before God's glory can be fully revealed.

Secondly, the Prophet saw the Lord. Throughout history, it has been the desire of many men of God to see the Lord. Moses requested God to show him His face. He so desired to look upon God's face; but he was only allowed to see God from behind, as He passed by the cleft of the rock. God told Moses that he would not live if he were to see His face. So he had to be satisfied with seeing only the rear view of God.

Now we read that the Prophet Isaiah saw the Lord. And he was terrified by what he saw:

> Then said I, Woe is me! For I am undone; because I am a man of unclean lips, and I dwell in the midst of a people of unclean lips: for mine eyes have seen the King, the LORD of hosts.
>
> *Isaiah 6:5*

The glory was too awesome. God's divine presence was nerve shattering and devastating. He could not stand the presence of such a Holy God. In fact, he wanted to die.

He could not be alive in God's holy presence. He saw the Lord and wanted to die. When we begin to experience God's holy presence in such an awesome manner, our flesh has to die. In fact, our flesh will die. When we see His face, we will want to die to everything which had been precious to us and treasured in our lives!

Thirdly, God was sitting upon a throne. The key point here is that the only true and living God of all creation was enthroned! God was enthroned! He has to be enthroned in our lives! This is the rightful place for Him to be. He should be in charge. He should be the one calling the shots! The throne is the rightful place for the King of kings and the Lord of lords! He wants to reign totally through us, from the throne of our hearts!

Fourth, God's throne was high and lifted up. Not only was His throne lifted up, it was also high. This speaks of the prominent status which is due to our God, and the respect and high honour due to Him.

This also confirms what the Scriptures say about our Lord Jesus in *Philippians 2:9*: "Wherefore God also hath highly exalted Him, and given Him a name which is above every name." He alone deserves all of the honour and the praise!

Jesus must be exalted and lifted up by our lifestyle of worship. He himself has declared, "And I, if I be lifted up from the earth, will draw all men unto me." (*John 12:32*)

Fifth, His train filled the temple. Looking upon the magnificent scene in his vision, Isaiah was overwhelmed by this awesome garment filling the whole temple. It was the train of the robe worn by the King. Even though His throne was high and lifted up, the train of His robe was so massive and gloriously enormous that it completely filled every nook and cranny of the Temple!

What an awesome sight! It was as though God's majesty, power and awesome glory were being exhibited in the huge train of His robe. God's Presence and Glory filled every part of the Temple. I can almost sense the dumbstruck awe Isaiah felt, as he experienced God's consuming Presence and Glory!

The Hem of His Garment

This reminds me of the story of the woman suffering from an issue of blood for 12 years. She said to herself, "If I may but touch His garment, I shall be whole" (*Matthew 9:21*). We read that, when she touched the hem of Jesus' garment, she was completely healed (*Matthew 9:20, 22*).

It was as if God was offering Isaiah a touch of the hem of His garment. I can almost hear Him say, "Isaiah, my servant, here's my train, the hem of my garment; just a touch will totally change your life forever!" There is enough power in the hem of His garment, the train of His robe, to completely heal, restore, revive and transform our lives. Hallelujah! The same power that was available to the sick woman and the Prophet Isaiah is still available to you and me today!

The Same Five Significant Elements

True worship contains these very same five elements that we observed in *Isaiah 6:1*. Our spirit has been awakened to those things that previously seemed insignificant; God the Holy Spirit has opened our eyes and minds to perceive things in a brand new way and to understand their significance.

1. "My king" in "my kingdom" needs to die. The things which I have enthroned in my life need to be dealt with effectively, absolutely and completely!

2. Once this happens, I will begin to see and experience "The Lord"! Since I have now prepared room for Him, He will want to come and remain with me.

3. God will take up residence in me, sitting upon "His Throne" in my life, where He rightfully belongs.

4. He will be high and lifted up in my daily living, in my worship, and in my praise and adoration.

5. His train will fill "this Temple"—me, my body, my life, my existence! I will be filled with a hunger and desire to become a 24/7 true worshipper.

As Isaiah continued to witness the process of worship, something happened to him that completely and forever revolutionized his life. Friend, when you and I enter into the holy presence of God, we will immediately realize our utter sinful state and start to confess and repent before God. God's holiness activates the realization of our true condition.

The holiness of God's presence caused Isaiah to confess and cry out to God in repentance, "Woe is me! For I am undone; because I am a man of unclean lips..." (*Isaiah 6:5*) No one can step into God's holy presence and remain the same. Under the conviction of the Holy Spirit, we will confess our sins and fall down before Him in repentance.

No human can stand in the holy presence of God. His holiness will consume us. His presence will kill us if we do not confess and repent. It is essential for our flesh to die when we enter His presence. Only when "I"—when "Self"— dies, disappears and evaporates, will God's holy presence begin to move in and take over.

Listen to Isaiah's confession. He cried and said, "*I* am undone." That's who "*I*" am. ***"I" am undone***. It is necessary to recognize and acknowledge who and what I am. I am undone. I am nothing. I am good for nothing. I am nobody. I am a sinner. I need God's grace, His mercy, His forgiveness, His favour.

During Isaiah's encounter with God, his major concern was that he would die. He cried out, "For mine eyes have seen the King, the Lord of hosts." No human can see God and live. God had to intervene so that the prophet would not die.

So God instructed a Seraphim to take a live coal from the altar and place it upon the Prophet's "unclean lips". The Seraphim then declared to him, "Thine iniquity is taken away, and thy sin purged." (*Isaiah 6:7*) The live coal of fire touching Isaiah's lips is a symbol of iniquity and sin being burnt and destroyed in his life. Only then, when his iniquity was forgiven and his sin purged, was he ready to be sent by God and used of God.

Holy service in God's Kingdom has to be preceded by honest confession, utter repentance, holy preparation, and true worship. In preparation for our ministry and mission, it is imperative that our sinful lips be touched by the live coal of fire from God's holy altar. Only then could the Prophet offer a clear response to God's call, "Whom shall I send, and who will go for us?" (*Isaiah 6:8a*) Isaiah was able to answer, "Here am I; send me." (*Isaiah 6:8b*) Only then was he ready and able to accept God's holy call upon his life.

Without Jesus, We Are Nothing

One day Jesus made this no-nonsense declaration: "For without me ye can do nothing." (*John 15:5*) He pulled no punches with this powerful, shocking statement.

He was straightforward, He was honest. In no uncertain terms, He made it plain and clear: without the grace and mercy of God, we are nothing. Nothing—not our abilities, nor our professional qualifications, nor our spiritual maturity, nor the esteemed positions we hold in society— nothing at all qualifies us for success without Jesus.

All of our achievements and capabilities bear absolutely no significance without the name of Jesus Christ. True worship is embracing that name, being enveloped by that name, being consumed by that name. Without Him we are nothing and can do nothing, but with Him we can do all things and we are capable of doing anything.

Paul the Apostle declared, "I can do all things through Christ which strengtheneth me." (*Philippians 4:13*) As true worshippers, we are able to excel in all facets of the Christian life because of our daily connection with Jesus our Master. We can confront challenges head-on and successfully deal with adversity and opposition in the name of Jesus Christ. We are able to step up and step forward with holy boldness and unwavering confidence, and win any battle. We are able to appropriately arrange life's priorities subject to the Word and the will of God.

Nothing else is of more importance to us than pleasing our Master. Experiencing true and holy worship of our Lord and Saviour becomes our top priority. The experience of the prophet Isaiah can thus become for us a daily reality.

Friend, is it your desire to experience true, glorious, holy worship every day? This marvellous experience is indeed possible and available to you and me right here, right now. Let us together enter into God's holy presence, just like the prophet Isaiah, and prepare ourselves for a glorious life-transforming encounter with the King of kings!

Let Us Pray

Please join me in this prayer:

My God and my Father, I come before you in the precious name of Jesus Christ, my Redeemer. As I bow before your throne in holy reverence of your awesome Majesty, I ask that you forgive me of all of my sin and iniquity.

Like the prophet Isaiah, I declare that I am undone, that I am a sinful man/woman of unclean lips, mind and heart, and that I live among a sinful people. Please forgive me of all my sin and iniquity; forgive me for failing to honour you in true worship; and for not obeying your commandments and your instructions, I ask your forgiveness.

I declare that without you I am nothing and without you I can do nothing. I need your forgiveness. I need your grace, your mercy, and your favour. Wash me, Lord, and cleanse me in the precious blood of your Son Jesus Christ, and grant me the opportunity to restore my worship relationship with you, my God and my Father.

I thank you for hearing my prayer and for helping me to become a 24/7 true worshipper. In Jesus' precious Name.

Amen.

CHAPTER FOUR

Thy Kingdom Come on Earth

As it is in Heaven

Jesus' main purpose for coming from Heaven to earth was to establish the Kingdom of God on earth. He proclaimed His mission clearly in a few statements He made while on earth. Firstly, He declared, "I must preach the kingdom of God... for therefore am I sent." (*Luke 4:43*) He also said, "For the Son of man is come to seek and to save that which was lost." (*Luke 19:10*)

John 3:16 records one of the most important statements in Scripture regarding His mission on earth: "For God so loved the world, that He gave His only begotten Son, that whosoever believeth in Him should not perish, but have everlasting life." Then, in *John 10:10*, Jesus gave His remarkable mission statement: "The thief cometh not, but for to steal, and to kill, and to destroy: I am come that they might have life, and that they might have it more abundantly."

One day, His disciples requested Him to teach them to pray. So He taught them the Lord's Prayer, as recorded in *Matthew 6:9-13*. Verse 10 reads: "Thy kingdom come, Thy will be done in earth, as it is in heaven." It is important to understand the contents of this prayer.

My understanding of the request made in verse 10 is as follows: we must ask the Father to transfer His heavenly Kingdom to the earth. We must ask that His will be duplicated on earth in the same manner as it is now observed in heaven. If my understanding is correct, then we ought to ascertain exactly what is now transpiring in heaven and request that it be transferred to the earth, so that God's kingdom may be established here.

This World Will Be a Different Place

When God's kingdom comes to the earth and His will is done here as it is in heaven, then this world will become a totally different place. God as King will reign, and He will be in charge of His Kingdom. The Bible tells us that in heaven there is no sin, sickness, disease, war, hatred, hunger, suffering or any other problem that people are experiencing on this earth. It is for this reason that God desires to transfer His heavenly Kingdom to earth.

John 3:16 gives us the clear message of God's agenda for the human race. It is His desire that everything be in perfect harmony with His will. It must be well with each and every person on the face of the earth. There should be no sin, sickness, disease, war, hatred, hunger or suffering on earth.

Our Presence Here On Earth

As God's Church, we should be making a difference to the sad situation on earth. Jesus said that we are the salt of the earth and the light of the world (*Matthew 5:13-14*). We should be God's ambassadors of goodwill on earth.

Our very presence on the earth should not only have a preservation impact, but also one of healing, renewal and restoration. Because of Jesus Christ in us, the world should have begun to experience God's greatness and His fullness through us. The bottom line is that God desires to establish His heavenly Kingdom on earth through us, His Church.

About the Seraphim

Coming back to the subject of worship in heaven, not much information is available in Scripture that would give us a clear idea as to what is transpiring there right now. The best account on this subject is found in Isaiah chapter 6, which we discussed in the previous chapter. It was as if God was offering the Prophet Isaiah a glimpse of what was happening around His throne 24/7.

We read about the strange creatures called Seraphim, continuously engaged in holy worship before God's throne. This was what they were calling out, one to the other without ceasing, over and over and over again: "Holy, holy, holy, is the LORD of hosts: the whole earth is full of His glory." (*Isaiah 6:3*)

We read that, when they cried out in holy worship, something happened within the Temple: "And the posts of the door moved at the voice of him that cried, and the house was filled with smoke." (*Isaiah 6:4*) It was then that the Prophet Isaiah came under conviction, realizing he was undone, unclean and sinful!

The continuous worship of the Seraphim was what caught my attention as I studied this holy scene: the act of worship as performed by them, and the manner in which they performed their ministry. The first thing I noticed was that worship before God's throne was all they did. They did nothing else but worshipped God continuously, crying out and proclaiming God's holiness to one another.

To me, it became clear that these creatures were specifically designed and created by God for the singular purpose of worship. Worship was their one and only task. God made them especially for this purpose. They were designed by the Master Creator for the purpose of worshipping Him alone.

God Created Different Angels

Different angelic beings were created by God for different tasks and assignments. The angel Gabriel was designed and created as a messenger angel. Any time God wanted to give a message to someone, Gabriel was the one dispatched to perform the assignment. He was the angel sent to Daniel in *Daniel 8:16*, and he brought the messages to Zacharias, the father of John the Baptist, and also to Mary, the mother of our Lord. Both incidents are recorded in Luke chapter 1.

Michael the Archangel was created to be a warrior angel. Every time there was warfare in the heavenlies, Michael was the General dispatched by God to execute the assignment, as recorded in *Revelation 12:7* and also in Daniel chapter 10.

It seems that Cherubim are angels created for the purpose of security, as recorded in *Genesis 3:24*. When God was instructing Moses on the design of the Ark of the Covenant, He directed Moses to make two cherubim and place them facing each other, one at each end of the Ark. The wings of the cherubim were to stretch out over the mercy seat and cover it (*Exodus 25:17-20*). These angels thus performed protective assignments at God's command.

Then there are several other kinds of angels created to carry out various assignments; among them are protective angels (*Psalm 91:11-12*), reaper angels (*Matthew 13:39*), and angels of wrath (*Acts 12:23*). But the Seraphim are different from these others; they are God's specially designed Creatures of Worship. They are always before His throne, engaged in continuous holy worship of God (*Isaiah 6*).

We will study the significance of the Seraphim's appearance and strange features in a later chapter—where the discoveries we make will lead to mind-boggling, life-changing revelations!

As It Is in Heaven

But, for now, let us return to the Lord's Prayer, where we are exhorted to request God to transfer the things in His heavenly Kingdom to the earth. What we must understand is that Heaven is God's dwelling place. He resides there. From there, He rules the universe. He is totally in charge there, and all of Heaven's activities are orchestrated and executed according to His divine will.

Nothing in heaven takes place outside of God's will. We need to be clear about this: that this order is what God envisages for the earth too. It is clear that God desires to see a world where His order rules the nations of the earth.

God's Priority for the Earth

God's will for the earth is that it be a place of love, peace, harmony and prosperity for all nations. We as humans need to understand the priority God places on our giving our full allegiance and loyalty to Him alone. He alone deserves our total respect and submission.

If, in answer to our prayers, the mode and ministry of 24/7 true worship is going to be transferred to earth, then surely the Seraphim—specifically created to perform this task—have to be part of this ministry on earth. God would therefore necessarily have to replicate the Seraphim on earth, in order for them to perform this ministry of "True Worship 24/7". Now, how will He manage to overcome this seemingly impossible challenge?

The Earthly Seraphim

Well, my friend, we know that with God nothing is impossible. In fact, He thrives on things thought impossible, Hallelujah! The solution to this problem is actually very simple. He is going to create this same Creature of Worship on earth. The Seraphim will worship Him right here on earth! But how will He manage to do this?

God will create a body for the Seraphim on earth. Spiritually, it will look exactly the same as the heavenly Seraphim. The body to be created is called "The Body of Christ" or "The People of God" or "The Church of Jesus Christ" or simply "God's Church". God will create this body with exactly the same features as the heavenly Seraphim.

Endowed with the Holy Spirit's Power

This divinely designed corporate body of believers will be God's representative on earth. It will be endowed with power from on high. It will be inspired from the very throne of Almighty God. God will fill this body with His Holy Spirit, His divine power, and His glory, thus enabling it to achieve even the impossible.

My mind goes back to the day Jesus made the following declaration, that "they will do even greater things than these, because I am going to the Father" (*John 14:12b, NIV*). Now He is offering us the power by which these greater works will be done. He promised, "But you shall receive power when the Holy Spirit has come upon you; and you shall be witnesses to Me in Jerusalem, and in all Judea and Samaria, and to the end of the earth" (*Acts 1:8, NKJV*)

Please note that this will be an earthly "Creature of Worship". It will be the heavenly Seraphim in an earthly body. The "Creature of Worship" will have "the image of a man". It will also have six wings, and it will have four faces. God will place a burning desire for worship inside of this creature. God will fill it with His Holy Spirit and with power.

49

This body will become God's Holy Temple, His earthly "Creature of Worship". This marvellous earthly Seraphim will want to worship God in spirit and in truth, 24/7. Not only will there be a burning desire to worship God, but worship will be mandatory. It will be a joyful, glorious and edifying experience. Continuous holy worship of God will be its only priority. God is going to utilize the ministry of this "Creature of Worship" to impact the nations of the earth.

Nations Touched, Changed and Set Free

God's earthly "Creature of Worship" will touch, influence and change nations around the world that have been struggling to connect to Him in various ways of worship. This creature will shake the foundations of the earth, for it has been specifically designed by God for this purpose.

In its act of true worship of Almighty God, it will move the posts of the door (*Isaiah 6:4a*). It will saturate the earth with the presence of the Lord, even as "the house was filled with smoke", as in Isaiah's vision (*Isaiah 6:4b*). Earthly kings and kingdoms will be moved and shaken, and the glory and knowledge of the Lord will fill the whole earth, as the waters cover the sea (*Isaiah 6:3, 11:9; Habakkuk 2:14*). Hallelujah!

I trust God that the Church will reach the point of truly understanding the powerful symbolism revealed in this glorious creature specifically designed for true worship. I do believe that, as the Holy Spirit reveals this message to hungry men and women of God across the globe, a powerful Holy Spirit revival will be ignited in many homes, churches and communities throughout the world.

The Huge Powerless Sleeping Giant

For too long, my friend, the Church of Jesus Christ has been like a huge, powerless sleeping giant, not knowing who or what it is supposed to be. Jesus said of the Church which He would build, that the gates of hell would not prevail against it! (*Matthew 16:18*) Well, as I look at today's Church, I notice Satan having a field day around the world.

Where is this powerful body of believers? Where is this glorious Church that is supposed to be God's authorized representative on earth? Where is God's mighty army? Taking a stand against the evil saturating this world? Sadly, no!

Evil in our communities is increasing by the hour, and Satan has become more blatant, daring and audacious. He is mocking and taunting God and His Church at every turn, with every facet of crudeness, vulgarity and daring indecency. But this giant, God's Church, is dead silent. God's people say nothing and do very little to change this unacceptable state of affairs in their communities.

Is it any wonder then that nations are dying by the millions of HIV, Aids and other horrendous sexually transmitted diseases? Young people are being systematically destroyed and killed right in front of our eyes, due to all kinds of abuse—drug abuse, alcoholism, sexual promiscuity and perversions. Gangs are prevalent in our schools, and boys and girls are forced to join these gangs. Our kids are taking drugs and dying younger and younger as a result of bad choices. Where will it all end?

Never before in history have we seen such a high rate of teenage pregnancies, with free "protected" sex becoming an acceptable practice throughout the world. Premarital sex has become a fully accepted norm in our society, against God's will. The sanctity of marriage and of the family unit has been totally disregarded. Children are suffering from the trauma of divorce. Rape, incest and sexual abuse of our children occur daily around the world, and nobody seems to be able to deal with this out-of-control situation.

In South Africa, the country of my birth, we have witnessed of late an unprecedented, dramatic increase in brutal rape of our precious babies. The statistics over the recent years have been staggering. Babies less than one month old are being raped by adults.

I heard a report of a new-born baby girl abandoned by its mother in a ditch with its umbilical cord still attached. A man who passed by the ditch saw the baby girl and decided to rape her. When he was done with his vile, despicable, horrendous deed, he simply left her in the ditch to die. Someone else passing by graciously took the child to the hospital. The last I heard, the baby was in a serious condition.

I wept when I heard this report. What is wrong with us? What has happened to the human species? Where will it end? Where lies the answer? Who can help us in this hour of desperation? Who can save our nations from destruction?

In the words of the song written by Andrea Crouch, "Jesus is the answer for the world today, above Him there's no other, Jesus is the way..." Jesus is the only Way. He has declared in *John 14:6*, "I am the way, the truth, and the life; no man cometh unto the Father, but by me."

He alone can change our world. The home needs to be the home God intended it to be, and marriage needs to be God-ordained marriage. The family needs to be the family unit God has designed and ordained it to be. The government needs to be a genuine government, doing what it is supposed to do, offering good governance of the country without bribery and corruption. The church needs to be "The Church", doing what God has designed and called it to be.

Let us join in prayer for God's Kingdom to come to earth, and for His will to be done on earth as it is in heaven. This world is desperately in need of divine intervention. We need Almighty God, we need His grace and mercy. God's Church needs to return to the place of true holy worship.

We, the Body of Christ, the Church of Jesus Christ, need to take up our role and responsibilities as God's earthly Seraphim. We need to engage in true holy worship of God, the only One who is able to change and save the nations of the world. Now is the time to repent. Now is the time to return. Now is the time to worship. Let us worship Almighty God in spirit and in truth!

CHAPTER FIVE

Designed for Worship

Six wings of the Seraphim, and hands
beneath their wings

The Seraphim, God's specially designed Creatures of Worship, have unique features. What marvellous beings! They look really strange and totally different from any other angels. Firstly, each has six wings, utilized for three different purposes: two wings to cover his face; two wings to cover his feet; and two wings for flying (*Isaiah 6:2*). Their strange bodies were full of eyes (*Revelation 4:6-8*), and they had hands underneath their wings (*Ezekiel 1:8*).

These are the very same creatures that were seen in a vision by the Prophet Ezekiel, as described in *Ezekiel 1:5-24*; and also by the Apostle John, the Revelator on the Isle of Patmos, as recorded in *Revelation 4:7-11*. These servants of God described the Seraphim's strange features as follows: they had the image of a man—the image of a human being. Ezekiel described their appearance as having "the likeness of a man" (*Ezekiel 1:5*).

They had four faces: the face of a man, the face of a lion, the face of an ox, and the face of an eagle (*Ezekiel 1:10; Revelation 4:7*). The first face of this Creature of Worship is a human face! With so many faces of so many creatures at His disposal, God chose to give the Seraphim a human face!

54

We will discuss the amazing significance of this in greater detail later in this book.

A Creature with Six Wings

First, let us take a look at the Seraphim's six wings. The Prophet Ezekiel reported that they had only four wings, but agreed on all the other features recorded in *Isaiah 6:2-4* and *Revelation 4:6-8*. Isaiah described for us the functions of the six wings, as he viewed them. He observed that the Seraphim used two wings to cover their faces and another two to cover their feet, and that they flew using the remaining two wings.

Two Wings Covering His Face

Firstly, each Seraphim covered his face with two wings. To me, it is clear that this was an act of reverence, honour and respect for God and for His holiness. As humans, we close our eyes when we enter God's presence or when we communicate with Him in prayer. But covering one's face goes beyond simply closing one's eyes; among other things, it symbolizes reverence, honour and respect.

Psychologically, this act indicates one who is trying to hide. It also conveys awe and a sense of unworthiness. So we see that, as the Seraphim is engaged in the act of worship before God's throne, he covers his face with two of his wings, thereby signifying his unworthiness, but also expressing awe, reverence and respect for the King of kings, who alone is worthy of worship. Hallelujah!

This should also be the attitude of anyone entering God's holy presence. Our sinful state should move us to want to cover our faces. An attitude of awe, reverence and respect for the King of kings and Lord of lords should be the modus operandi when we come before Him in holy worship. But, many times, our attitude leaves much to be desired because we seem to forget who and what we are.

We should at all times approach God's holy presence with the attitude that "I am nothing" and "I am an unworthy servant". The attitude of John the Baptist, the forerunner of Jesus Christ, is the one to emulate. The humility of this down-to-earth servant of God is evidenced by his assertion, "He [Jesus] must increase, but I must decrease" (*John 3:30*), and further confirmed when he said he was unworthy to even untie the shoelaces of Jesus Christ (*Luke 3:16*).

Please allow me at this juncture to make the following statement: ***I believe the greatness of any servant of God is reflected in the smallness of his or her ego.*** When you and I can reach the point where we totally disappear in God's holy presence, cover our faces and become absolutely nothing, it is then that we can become the most powerful force in the universe.

The fact of the matter is that the heart of true worship is all about HIM and nothing about me. HE IS EVERYTHING and I am absolutely NOTHING. The greatest Christians on earth are the ones who can learn from this powerful example of the Seraphim.

Cover up in reverence and respect. Disappear. Become a zero in God's holy presence. Let us become nothing and allow God to make something great of you and me. God's Holy Spirit will saturate our whole being when we are able to completely submit to Him and to His precious will.

Two Wings Covering His Feet

Secondly, the Prophet Isaiah noticed the Seraphim using two wings to cover his feet. It is amazing how important the feet are to God. In his encounter with God, Moses was instructed to take the shoes off his feet, for God had declared the place where he stood to be holy ground. This same Prophet Isaiah also made the following glorious pronouncement:

> How beautiful upon the mountains are the feet of him that bringeth good tidings, that publisheth peace; that bringeth good tidings of good, that publisheth salvation; that saith unto Zion, Thy God reigneth!
>
> *Isaiah 52:7*

To me, the feet in Scripture represent the Ministry Gifts received from God to fulfil our assignments. Notice that the Seraphim covered his feet with two of his wings. In the presence of God, not only do I become nothing, but also my gifts and abilities become absolutely zero.

According to *James 1:17*, God is the Giver of every good and perfect gift. I dare not boast or brag about any of my gifts, talents, ministries or abilities before the throne of Him who graciously blessed me with them. In His holy presence, all of our good and perfect ministries and gifts become as nothing. So they have to be covered.

The example set by the Seraphim, of covering his feet with two of his wings, should be emulated by all who have been blessed by God with gifts and ministries. What we see here truly is mind boggling. Firstly we see reverence, honour and respect for the Giver of all good and perfect gifts; and then we see reverence, honour and respect for the gifts received from the Giver. Do we truly grasp and understand the awesome symbolism represented here, my friend?

Whoever we are, or think we are, let it be clear that we are nothing and we have nothing when we enter God's holy presence. We simply become a big fat ZERO in the presence of God, the Creator of the universe. So let us rid ourselves of our huge egos and of any idea that somehow makes us imagine we are something special in God's Kingdom.

Actually we are nothing. We have absolutely nothing. Now, let's cover up. Let us cover our faces and our feet, because we are in the presence of an awesome holy God. We need to realize that God alone is great, awesome, marvellous, wonderful, beautiful and glorious! To Him alone belongs the Kingdom, the power and the glory, forever and ever, Amen!

With Two Wings He Could Fly

Thirdly, the Prophet noticed the Seraphim using two wings for the purpose for which wings were originally designed. Wings were made to fly. God in His divine wisdom designed wings for all flying creatures. This means that the Seraphim has the ability to rise and elevate himself beyond the reach of anyone and anything at any given time.

The Seraphim can fly. The Creature of Worship is able to fly! Please let me repeat: the Creature of Worship is able to fly!

Now, to come back to us—God's Church, God's people. God has given His body, His church, His people the ability to fly. You are wondering how we can fly? You and I, my friend, have the ability to face opposition, challenges and obstacles, and we are able to deal with them in the name of Jesus Christ. But there will be times when we may reach a point where we just need to take a break and get away for a while.

Well, that is when we are able to spread our wings and fly. As the Psalmist David put it: "Oh, that I had wings like a dove! For then would I fly away, and be at rest." (*Psalm 55:6*) Friend, we have the ability to rise up above any problem, circumstance or difficulty, and fly away!

We Can Fly!

We have been given wings to fly. We are able to stand firm and strong in any adverse situation and still come out on top. My dear friend, we have been endowed with some amazing abilities we may not even know we possess! We have an inner strength, a tenacity that enables us to face difficulties, challenges and even tragedies, and to overcome the odds.

It is often not easy to deal with challenges but, if we try hard enough, we will even surprise ourselves and those around us. Let us be encouraged by the Apostle Paul, who declared, "In all these things we are more than conquerors through Him that loved us" (*Romans 8:37*).

59

Let us also join Paul in affirming that "I can do all things through Christ which strengtheneth me" (*Philippians 4:13*). Yes my friend, we can fly! You can fly! I can fly!

There is a song written and performed by a singer named R. Kelly which goes: "I believe I can fly; I believe I can touch the sky; I think about it every night and day; spread my wings and fly away..." God has given His Creature of Worship two wings with which to fly!

Are you facing problems or difficulties today? Is there something pulling you down or holding you down? Well, why don't you simply spread those powerful wings of yours and fly away? Rise up above your circumstances and difficulties! Remember, friend, you can fly! Right here, right now! Come on, let's go! Let's fly in Jesus' name! Hallelujah!

They Had Hands beneath Their Wings

We read in *Ezekiel 1:8* that the creatures had hands beneath their wings. I believe the hands represent instruments of service. We too have been blessed with hands with which to perform our daily tasks. We do most of our work with our hands. Hands are very important because they enable us to live a productive life.

God has specifically blessed the human species with hands and feet. Have you ever paused to think about this interesting fact? No other species has been blessed in this manner. Most of them have a head, eyes, ears, mouth and legs. But humans are the only ones blessed with hands.

Of our five senses—taste, hearing, sight, smell and touch—I believe that touch is one of the most important. Because, even though one may be blind or deaf or not able to smell or taste anything, every one of us is still able to feel and touch with our hands.

Even animals have the sense of touch, but only humans have these marvellous tools of service called hands. Why don't you pause now for a minute and just look at your hands? You are looking at a pair of anointed instruments of service and worship created by Almighty God. This is what they are meant to be and do. How beautiful and significant they are!

What would we do without them? Other people would then have to do things for us. But they are important not only for work. More especially, they are important for worship. Hands have featured predominantly in Scripture when it comes to worship. God has designed our hands for the special purpose of service to Him and to our fellow humans.

What would you say: that we have hands because we are human, or that we are human because we have hands? In my view, both statements would be correct, because the one complements the other. The Bible teaches that we worship and praise Almighty God by lifting up our hands to Him (*Psalms 28:2 & 63:4; 1 Timothy 2:8*). Then, throughout Scripture, we see the laying on of hands to bless (*Mark 10:16; Matthew 19:15*), to minister healing (*Mark 16:18; Acts 9:17 & 28:8*), and in the ordination and consecration of servants of God (*Acts 6:6; 1 Timothy 4:14*).

Without fear of contradiction, we can say that our hands are our God-given instruments of service and worship. It is therefore in our interest to study the hands beneath the wings of the Seraphim, as this Creature of Worship has been given hands for the purposes of service and worship too.

I think you will agree that, since humans are the only species on earth endowed by God with hands, the hands beneath the wings of the Seraphim have to be of prophetic significance to us. Isaiah witnessed the Seraphim using his hand to remove a burning coal from the altar with tongs and to touch the prophet's lips with it (*Isaiah 6:6-7*). In this manner, Isaiah's sins were purged and he was forgiven.

God desires to be worshipped in spirit and in truth. We worship Him with uplifted hands. In this way, we submit to Him, and we give honour and reverence to the KING of kings and the LORD of lords.

John the Revelator Saw the Same Creature

In the book of Revelation, we discover that John, the New Testament prophet, was also privileged to witness this amazing Creature of Worship. John's description of the vision he saw is truly mind-boggling:

> I looked, and, behold, a door was opened in heaven: and the first voice which I heard was as it were of a trumpet talking with me; which said, Come up hither, and I will shew thee things which must be hereafter. And immediately I was in the spirit: and, behold, a throne was set in heaven, and one sat on the throne.
>
> *Revelation 4:1-2*

Please note, my dear friend, that John saw exactly the same scene witnessed by Isaiah and Ezekiel. It was as if he was watching a repeat performance of God's heavenly proceedings.

John described God's appearance on His holy throne as "like [the crystalline sparkle of] a jasper stone and [the fiery redness of] a sardius stone"; and "encircling the throne there was a rainbow that looked like [the colour of an] emerald" (*Revelation 4:3, AMP*). Wow! How awesome!

Then he saw around the throne twenty-four seats and upon those seats sat twenty-four elders clothed in white robes, and each of them were wearing a golden crown on his head. Out of the throne proceeded lightning and thunder and voices, and there were seven lamps of fire burning before the throne. Those seven lamps represented the seven Spirits of God. Before the throne was what looked like a sea of crystal glass, and around the throne stood the four Creatures of Worship. (*Revelation 4:4-6*)

John noticed something else about the appearance of those creatures that was not mentioned by either Isaiah or Ezekiel. He saw that they were full of eyes, front and rear. With this amazing feature, they could look everywhere at all times. It was as if they would never be caught off guard, because of their 360-degree vision.

With the precious Holy Spirit as our Leader and Guide moment by moment, we have been endowed with this same feature too. So, we should also be always on the alert and never be caught off guard, as we move under God's holy anointing, led by the Holy Spirit (*1 John 2:20*).

The creatures had four different faces. Each one had a different face. One had the face of a Man, another the face of a Lion, the third the face of what he calls "a calf" or an Ox, and the fourth creature had the face of an Eagle. Each of them had six wings. (*Revelation 4:7-8*)

John noticed that those creatures never rested, day or night. They were constantly and continually engaged in 24/7 worship before God's holy throne, proclaiming, "Holy, holy, holy, LORD God Almighty, which was, and is, and is to come." (*Revelation 4:8*) Now, something fantastic happened when those creatures engaged in holy worship.

Each time they did so, the twenty-four elders fell down before Him who sat on the throne and cast their golden crowns before the throne. At the same time, they declared:

> Thou art worthy, O Lord, to receive glory and honour and power: for Thou hast created all things, and for Thy pleasure they are and were created.
>
> *Revelation 4:11*

Further on, we read that they were joined by a massive combined chorus of every creature in heaven and on earth, and under the earth, and all that is in the sea. And this enormous choir proclaimed with one voice:

> Blessing, and honour, and glory, and power, be unto Him that sitteth upon the throne, and unto the Lamb for ever and ever.
>
> *Revelation 5:13*

What a glorious sight! What awesome majesty, what marvellous power, what absolute glory belongs to our Father God! He truly is our Father and our God, the one and only Creator worthy of worship and praise!

My friend, please agree with me in prayer right now, as I sense God's holy anointing and amazing, awesome presence!

> *Heavenly Father, help us right now to realize and recognize what an awesome God you are. Help us, Lord, to take charge of our circumstances, to open our wings, and to soar up above them to new heights of victory. In Jesus' glorious name, Amen!*

Right now, my friend, why not offer the Lord your worship, praise, adoration, and thanks for victories in your life?

CHAPTER SIX

The Four Faces of the Seraphim

Man, Lion, Ox and Eagle

The Face of a Man
(Dominion)

First of all, I find it truly amazing that God has given this awe inspiring Creature of Worship the likeness of a man (*Ezekiel 1:5*) and the face of a man (*Ezekiel 1:10*). God's Creature of Worship bears the mark of a human being. There is an element of humanity built into this marvellous being.

Man, in God's creation plan, represents the culmination of creation, and man bears God's mark of perfection, intellect and dominion:

> God said, Let us make man in our image, after our likeness: and let them have dominion... over all the earth... So God created man in His own image, in the image of God created He him...
>
> *Genesis 1:26-27*

Man bears God's mark. God's image. God's likeness. How awesome! We bear God's mark. We bear God's image. We bear God's likeness. We are the glorious crown of God's creation. Now we can better understand why God's Creature of Worship has the likeness of a man and the face of a man!

Why the face of a man?

Our awe and wonder can find no better expression than through the words of Job:

> What is man, that Thou shouldest magnify him? And that Thou shouldest set Thine heart upon him?
>
> *Job 7:17*

King David follows up by asking:

> What is man, that Thou art mindful of him? And the son of man, that Thou visitest him?
>
> For Thou hast made him a little lower than the angels, and hast crowned him with glory and honour.
>
> Thou madest him to have dominion over the works of Thy hands; Thou hast put all things under his feet.
>
> *Psalm 8:4-6*

How awesome! These declarations of man's authority and dominion over God's creation, conferred on him as God's representative on earth, give us a better understanding of man's role in the earthly function of worship.

Even though Man was a failure, God still chose to use him

> And God saw that the wickedness of man was great in the earth, and that every imagination of the thoughts of his heart was only evil continually.
>
> And it repented the LORD that He had made man on the earth, and it grieved Him at His heart.
>
> *Genesis 6:5-6*

Even though man originally failed in the purpose for which he had been created, God has been unrelenting in His pursuit to bring him back to his rightful position—that of being a "Creature of Worship". But first, God had to deal with man's sin and failure, by removing him from his originally assigned position of earthly ruler and true worshipper.

Man had to be taught a hard lesson. He would be disciplined by his Father. He was destined to learn that God is serious about His Word. There would be forgiveness if he repented, and there would be restoration if he was willing to return and submit to his Creator. So, even though man's fallibility in the combined areas of disobedience, vanity and insecurity has been confirmed, God in His infinite mercy still offers grace and forgiveness to those who repent and turn from their wicked ways.

This is why the first face of the Seraphim is the face of a man. This is the original face of the Seraphim, the original face of God's "Creature of Worship". Man will be reconnected to his Creator when he understands and accepts the purpose for which he has been created.

The Face of a Lion
(Authority and Royalty)

The second face of the Seraphim is the face of a Lion. The Lion represents Authority and Royalty. Since time immemorial, the Lion has been respected and revered as king over the animal kingdom.

A Lion's appearance evokes different emotions within a person. On the one hand, the Lion's face bears a kind of strange, elegant beauty. On the other hand, it strikes a chord of fear into anyone facing this awesome creature. When you look into those scary eyes, you realize that their main purpose is to intimidate the Lion's adversaries.

A Lion commands reverence and respect. Without doing anything, it somehow seems to be saying, "Look at me, fear me, revere me, respect me, honour me, I am the king, I bear the mark of royalty..."

The Lion of Judah

While John the Revelator was on the isle of Patmos, he saw a vision of Almighty God seated on His throne in heaven (*Revelation 4*). As he continued to witness what was happening in this vision, the following scene took place:

> And I saw in the right hand of Him that sat on the throne a book... And no man in heaven, nor in earth, neither under the earth, was able to open the book, neither to look thereon.
>
> And I wept much, because no man was found worthy to open and to read the book, neither to look thereon.
>
> And one of the elders saith unto me, Weep not: behold, **the Lion of the tribe of Judah**, the Root of David, hath prevailed to open the book, and to loose the seven seals thereof.
>
> *Revelation 5:1, 3-5*

The Lion of Judah is KING! Jesus is KING!

Now, listen to what the Apostle Peter declared to the Church:

> But ye are a chosen generation, a royal priesthood, an holy nation, a peculiar people; that ye should shew forth the praises of Him who hath called you out of darkness into His marvellous light.
>
> *1 Peter 2:9*

We are a royal priesthood. We, as God's Church, bear the mark of royalty and authority. Jesus has declared, "All authority in heaven and on earth has been given to me" (*Matthew 28:18, NIV*), and this authority He has also given to us, His Church:

> "Behold, I give you the authority to trample on serpents and scorpions, and over all the power of the enemy, and nothing shall by any means hurt you."
>
> *Luke 10:19, NKJV*

The Lion has been endowed with authority and royalty. The Lion needs to roar! When the Lion begins to roar in the jungle, it demonstrates authority. Its prey takes note. The beasts fear; they scatter and scamper away into their hiding places. The Creature of Worship has the face of a Lion. It needs to demonstrate its authority over its environment.

This Lion, the Church of Jesus Christ, needs to roar. It needs to let the world hear its mighty roar:

> Cry aloud, spare not, lift up thy voice like a trumpet, and shew my people their transgression, and the house of Jacob their sins.
>
> *Isaiah 58:1*

The Church needs to make itself heard in all segments of society, to roar its disapproval of the evil perpetuated in our communities and in nations around the world. It needs to roar in the face of anti-God, anti-Christ humanistic propagation and acceptance of ungodly and evil practices.

The Lion needs to roar in God's Church, wherever unscriptural and ungodly practices are perpetuated, accepted and defended. It needs to roar against church leaders who have openly adopted the way and error of Balaam (*Jude 11*). It needs to roar where money, fame and fortune have become the gods now being openly worshipped.

It is time for the Lion to roar against the prevalence and amicable acceptance of sexual immorality and adulterous and promiscuous behaviour even among God's people and church leaders today. The Lion needs to roar against the increase of all kinds of addictions, including alcoholism, drug addiction, and gambling that is prevalent even among church leaders and church members.

May I ask you a question? If our Master is called "the Lion of the tribe of Judah"; if our Daddy is this Majestic Lion; then who and what are we His children supposed to be?

Yes, my friend, it is time for the Lion to roar in the name of Jesus Christ; so that we, His people, will humble ourselves and pray, repent, seek God's face, and turn from our wicked ways (*2 Chronicles 7:14*). We need to turn to God for His grace and mercy. We need to return to our rightful position and prostrate ourselves before God's throne in true holy worship. Yes Sir, the Lion, the Church has to roar! Roar in Jesus' name! Roar today! Roar now! Loud and clear!

The Face of an Ox
(Service, Servanthood, Tenacity and Endurance)

The third face of the Seraphim, God's Creature of Worship, is the face of an Ox. The Ox is possibly one of the least interesting and least understood animals, about which very little is known or documented. It seems that very few people have ever bothered to take a closer look at this astounding creature. But the Ox really is an exceptional animal.

It was created to be a powerful beast of burden, a strong working animal. Very few animals can rival the Ox when it comes to carrying or pulling heavy loads. The raw strength, power and toughness of this creature truly is unparalleled.

The other unique feature of the Ox is its relationship with its owner. The Ox exists simply to please its owner. Its total joy and pleasure is found in pleasing its owner. Though not generally regarded as an intelligent beast, the Ox has certain unique qualities of its own.

The Ox knows its owner

Hear, O heavens, and give ear, O earth: for the LORD hath spoken, I have nourished and brought up children, and they have rebelled against me.

The ox knoweth his owner... but Israel doth not know, my people doth not consider.

Isaiah 1:2-3

It is interesting that God should use the Ox as a role model when He made His point about His people's callous attitude towards Him, their Owner. The Ox's devotion to its owner is well proven. Of all the animals known for their obedience and submission to their owner, the Ox probably tops the list.

The Ox knows its owner. The Ox may not be as intelligent as some other animals, but one thing about it is clear. God says, "The Ox knows its Owner." The Ox knows and identifies with the needs of its owner. It is willing to submit to those needs and fulfil them, whatever the cost. Because it knows its owner and the job that needs to be done, it is willing to be its owner's complete slave. It is 100 percent committed and dedicated to the exclusive service of its owner 24/7.

Very few animals can keep up with the sheer brute strength and tenacity of the Ox when it comes to productivity and service. Here is an animal willing and able to work continuously 24/7 until the job is done.

The Ox takes pleasure in service

It seems that the key to the Ox's total commitment is the pleasure and satisfaction it derives from the devoted service it renders to its owner. One can almost hear it say, "Give me some more, stack it high, add more weight, I can take some more, give me longer working hours!"

Its absolute dedication, dependability and longsuffering, and its contentment in serving its master, are some of the outstanding inherent qualities of this amazing beast. Its endurance and its tenacious nature make the Ox a truly outstanding and hardworking creature of service. For the Ox, there is no room for half-hearted service where its master is concerned. It is totally sold out to rendering quality service to its master 24/7.

Bear one another's burdens
(Be an Ox for God)

Are you an Ox for God? Do you have what it takes? This, my friend, is where the rubber meets the road. Can God depend on us? Can you and I offer our lives and commit ourselves to complete 24/7 service to our Master, without counting the cost?

When Paul the Apostle declared, "I bear in my body the marks of the Lord Jesus" (*Galatians 6:17*), he was actually saying, "I am an Ox for Christ."

Paul also said, "Bear ye one another's burdens, and so fulfil the law of Christ" (*Galatians 6:2*). Are you ready and willing to bear the burdens of others in the Body of Christ? Are you committed to be an Ox for Christ by serving His Body?

Jesus one day set an astonishing qualification for those who would follow Him, when He said, "And whosoever doth not bear his cross, and come after me, cannot be my disciple" (*Luke 14:27*).

Wow! What a statement! Can you take it? Are you really willing to become an Ox for God?

This is the call from God's throne when He looks for true worshippers. God is looking for Oxen: those willing to commit their lives 100 percent to their Master and serve Him 24/7 in true worship. Are you willing and able to say yes to our Master and pay the price of total service to Him?

The Face of an Eagle
(Vision, Strength and Agility)

We now come to the fourth face of the Seraphim: the face of an Eagle. As we look at this glorious winged creature, the very first trait we notice about it is that it never flies in flocks. Most birds fly in flocks, but Eagles fly alone. At no time anywhere has anybody witnessed a flock of Eagles. Why? Because Eagles always fly alone.

An Eagle is never dependent on any of its fellow Eagles for its existence, simply because it is totally dependent on the provision supplied by God, its Creator. The independent nature of the Eagle is qualified and perfected by its dependence upon God's provision.

Another remarkable feature about the Eagle is that it is possibly one of the most perfectly designed birds in creation. Its majestic wingspan of almost four meters across, together with its super aerodynamic body, makes it perfectly balanced for both flying very high or simply soaring on air currents.

The Eagle epitomises strength, endurance and agility. In a message delivered through the Prophet Isaiah, God exhorted His people to wait upon Him, promising them that they would soar like eagles if they did so:

> But they that wait upon the Lord shall renew their strength; they shall mount up with wings as eagles; they shall run, and not be weary; and they shall walk, and not faint.
>
> *Isaiah 40:31*

God stirs up our nest

There are more references made in Scripture to the Eagle than to any other bird. In the book of Deuteronomy, for instance, God used the example of the Eagle to give us some insights into how He cared for His people, Israel:

> As an eagle stirreth up her nest, fluttereth over her young, spreadeth abroad her wings, taketh them, beareth them on her wings: So the LORD alone did lead him, and there was no strange god with him.
>
> *Deuteronomy 32:11-12*

The eagle's way of raising and training her young is probably one of the most impressive in nature. There is a time for nurturing, caring and protecting her babies. But then the time comes for the young eaglets, now about three years old, to grow up and leave the nest—even, if necessary, to be evicted by force!

God says that this is the same method He uses to nurture His people. He sometimes has to evict us from our cosy, comfortable little nests and make us go out there to face challenges. It is only in so doing that we—like the eaglets—can grow to become the Creatures of Worship that God intended us to be.

Another point that God made—and He made it very clearly—was that He *alone* led His people: "there was no strange god" with them (*Deuteronomy 32:12*). Almighty God was the only One whom they worshipped.

The Eagle's vision

It is the tremendous strength of the Eagle's wings that enables it to fly to enormous heights. Most of us would say that this is its most outstanding ability: the capacity to reach amazing heights. Well, we would be almost correct, but the Eagle has another even more exceptional feature, one that surpasses its powers of flight. This is its Vision.

No other bird possesses the incomparable, superlative vision of the Eagle. Flying at a height of about one kilometre in the air, it is able to spot its prey—a rabbit, a rat, or even a mouse—on the ground. This feat would be simply impossible for any other bird of prey to accomplish. God said to Job:

> Doth the eagle mount up at thy command, and make her nest on high? She dwelleth and abideth on the rock, upon the crag of the rock, and the strong place. From thence she seeketh the prey, and her eyes behold afar off.
>
> *Job 39:27-29*

Yes, God created the Eagle with absolute, perfect, far-seeing vision! We need to have perfect vision and foresight too, to be able to deal with today's challenges. The Word of God teaches us, "Where there is no vision, the people perish!" (*Proverbs 29:18*) Clear, unobstructed vision is a prerequisite in the Church today, if we are to have any success in fulfilling our God-given assignment. We must be able to see the things the Holy Spirit wants to reveal to us. Our spiritual eyes need to be opened to see clearly the needs around us and the challenges and opportunities before us.

We need to clearly see Satan's deceptions; to clearly see the evil, sin, iniquity and corruption all around us. God's Creatures of Worship should start employing their gift of vision. Let us submit to Him now, for without vision we will surely perish. Let us agree with the hymn writer, Clara Scott:

> Open my eyes that I may see
> Glimpses of truth Thou hast for me;
> Place in my hands the wonderful key
> That shall unclasp and set me free.
>
> — *From the hymn, "Open My Eyes" by Clara Scott*

God has marvellous and important things He wants to show us. We need to utilize the exceptional gift of vision that comes with the leadership of the Holy Spirit. We need to lead the Church back to the place of true worship and total dedication.

The eagle is monogamous
(Faithful to only one mate for life)

The Eagle possesses another amazing trait that is unknown to most people. I too was unaware of this outstanding characteristic until I started studying this majestic bird. Let me tell you that, when I learnt about this exemplary quality exhibited by the Eagle, I had to drop my head in shame and weep before God on behalf of the entire human race.

My friend, the Eagle is monogamous. It has only one mate throughout its entire life. It marries only once, and that's it! It stays with its mate for the rest of its life. This in itself should be a lesson on successful marriage relationships for us!

Another discovery about the Eagle is that it makes its home in the same nest for its entire life. As nesting time approaches, the Eagle simply builds further on its existing nest, making it bigger, more spacious and more comfortable. Black Eagles have been known to keep the same nest for up to 70 years. How impressive!

The Eagle stays with its original mate for life and keeps the original nest for the whole of its life. Wow! My, oh my! My friend, what an awesome lesson for us humans! May God help us! For centuries we have been struggling so hard to make a success of our marriages and family relationships.

We are still struggling daily to try to make things work, because we have opted for the easiest way out to solve our problems. Our solution to marital and relationship problems is to give up on the other person and say, "Let's break up. Let's separate. Let's get divorced." And yet, even after the separation and divorce, we still continue to struggle.

Well, my friend, I think God has something very important to teach us from the life of this magnificent creature. We would gain much wisdom if we could take serious note of the excellent example set by this noble bird.

Dear friend, not only does the Seraphim have the face of a Man, the face of a Lion, and the face of an Ox, it also has the face of an Eagle. Four faces, representing the traits of four glorious creatures combined into one.

Four Creatures Fused into One "Creature of Worship"

What a strange and unusual, yet marvellous combination! Only God Almighty in His infinite wisdom is able to create such an awesome being for His divine pleasure! To have the traits, qualities and abilities of four exceptional creatures moulded and united into one body really is remarkable.

The Seraphim, God's designated Creature of Worship, has been replicated in the Body of Christ, God's Church on earth. We are His Creatures of Worship on earth.

We, His Church, do have the face of a Man and man's dominion over creation conferred on us by Almighty God. Then we have the face of a Lion, challenging us to take up the mantle of Authority and Royalty endowed on us by God. Thirdly, we have the face of an Ox, demanding from us dedication, commitment and tenacity in our service to our Master. And, finally we, have the face of an Eagle, exhorting us to take hold of this powerful bird's vision, strength and agility with which to do our task.

You and I, my friend, are God's Creatures of Worship! All we need to do is to submit ourselves to His call and accept this awesome responsibility. Jesus has said that God is searching for such people, who will worship Him in spirit and in truth.

So, today, please allow me to share with you the good news: the next time anyone accuses you of being two-faced, you may take the liberty to correct that person. Please let them know that you are in fact not two-faced, but four-faced!

Now, my friend, are you ready to accept this wonderful assignment? Are you ready and willing to join God's mighty, powerful army of true worshippers? Are you? Will you? If so, then come on. Let's go in Jesus' Name!

With God's holy anointing upon me, I feel like praying right now. Please join me in prayer:

Dear God, precious Heavenly Father, on behalf of the millions across the world, I drop my head in shame and repentance. I weep for the many thousands of broken homes, broken marriages, broken communities, and broken nations throughout the world.

Father, we have failed dismally in all of our efforts, simply because of our pride and hardheartedness. We have broken that which you have created. We have defiled that which you have sanctified and ordained as holy. We have caused so many innocent souls to suffer because of our hardness of heart. Lord, please forgive us. Forgive us our pride and our unforgiving attitudes.

Help us, Lord, to return to you; to come back to the place where you can change us for eternity. All this I ask in the precious name of Jesus Christ our risen Lord.

Amen.

CHAPTER SEVEN

Apostasy and Abominations

Hindrances to revival and true worship

Throughout Scripture, Almighty God has made it very clear that He wants to dwell among His people. He desires to have a close relationship with us; this has been His quest ever since man's fall in the Garden of Eden. God has not quit on man. For a very long time, He has been trying to bring us back to the place where the broken relationship between man and Himself can be restored.

Because of His love for us and His uncompromising commitment to restoring this original relationship, God has persisted in His pursuit of man. Speaking through the Old Testament Prophets—Moses, Samuel, Isaiah, Jeremiah, Ezekiel, Daniel, among many others—He has constantly been calling us back to Himself.

Instead of heeding God's urgent call, however, our forefathers chose to ignore Him. They even killed many of these prophets. But, in spite of the opposition and danger they faced, all of these servants of God remained faithful and true to their God-given message. They did not in any manner waver in fulfilling their assignments.

God's Efforts through the Ages

Right up to the last Old Testament prophet, Malachi, God was calling His people to repent and return to Him. When they did not, His final word to them was crystal clear:

> For, behold, the day cometh, that shall burn as an oven; and all the proud, yea, and all that do wickedly, shall be stubble: and the day that cometh shall burn them up, saith the LORD of hosts...
>
> *Malachi 4:1*

In the very last verse in the Old Testament, in Malachi 4:6b, God issued a final word to man to repent, "lest I come and smite the earth with a curse." God has always remained faithful in His love, grace and mercy towards us. But, when we constantly and continually reject Him and wilfully ignore His pleas to us to return to Him, then only one last option remains. Like any good father who loves his child dearly, God has to discipline and punish His children.

All throughout Old Testament times, man had been saying "no" to the call of God. Then Father God had to adopt "Plan B" in an effort to still reach out to save the people He loved so dearly. His people. He would send His only begotten Son to earth. He would be willing to dispatch to earth the one most dear to Him. To let that Son suffer and die as a sacrifice for the redemption of the human race.

So Jesus came to earth as a babe, born in a stable through a lowly virgin. But, when He arrived, the "Church" of the day and its leaders failed to recognize, acknowledge or accept Him as their Messiah and Saviour.

Jesus Was Rejected and Despised

Jesus the Son of God was rejected, despised, ridiculed and hated by the church leaders of His time. They thought they knew God and tried to convince people they really knew what they were doing. But, in retrospect, we now know that they were only playing church. Pretending to be serving Almighty God.

They imposed on people a kind of powerless man-made Religion that did nothing for anyone but only served to inflate their own already-bloated egos. They did not really know the God whom they professed to be serving. So, in their ignorance of the truth and to satisfy the "church board" of the day, they decided to get rid of this "false prophet" named Jesus. They did not want Him making inroads into their religious territory or converting their followers. So they decided to kill Him.

Please note, my friend, it was the church leaders who rejected Jesus. They, the ones who supposedly served Jehovah God, came up with the plot to kill Jesus. Not the sinners, or the publicans, or the harlots, or the prostitutes, or the drunkards, or the hooligans. No, it was the leaders of the Church!

Why did they do it, you may ask? Because they did not really know God. They never knew Him. Therefore, they did not really know Jesus. Like so many of us today. We profess to know Jesus, and we think we know Him, but we simply do not know Him. We may have heard of Him, and we may even know much about Him. But we do not really KNOW HIM!

These people, like their forefathers, were in fact also saying "No" to God when they said "No" to Jesus. They were in effect saying, "No, we don't want you"; "No, we don't need you." So they killed Him. But, after His resurrection and before He left to return to His Father in heaven, Jesus gave His disciples a marvellous promise. He promised to send them the Holy Spirit, who would teach, lead and guide them into all truth and righteousness.

A further important work of the Holy Spirit is to convict us of sin and iniquity. Following God's first two initiatives to bring man back to Himself, this would be His final attempt. First we said "No" to God the Father, then we said "No" to His Son Jesus Christ. It now seems that this would be God's last and final effort to get us back, and man's last and final chance to heed God's call to return to Him.

After this, there is nothing more God can do for the human race. It is as if God's resources for man's salvation have now become depleted. After the Holy Spirit, there is nothing more He can do for us. If now, for the third time, we decide to say "No" to Him by rejecting the Holy Spirit, there is nothing else He can do for us.

What if We Reject the Holy Spirit?

Jesus made this shocking statement one day, when He was speaking about the Holy Spirit:

Wherefore I say unto you, All manner of sin and blasphemy shall be forgiven unto men: but the blasphemy against the Holy Ghost shall not be forgiven unto men.

And whosoever speaketh a word against the Son of man, it shall be forgiven him: but **whosoever speaketh against the Holy Ghost, it shall not be forgiven him, neither in this world, neither in the world to come**.

Matthew 12:31-32

My dear friend, when we say "no" to the Holy Spirit, we are effectively cutting ourselves off from God's grace, mercy and salvation. Why? Because God has offered us His best and His last. He has nothing else to give us that would save us from the destruction of hell. Jesus says that, when we speak against the Holy Spirit, there will be no forgiveness in this life or in eternity.

Wow! What an amazing declaration! What a serious warning! We need to be very careful that we do not, in our egoistic, humanistic manner, refuse the Holy Spirit (*Hebrews 3:7-8*), grieve Him (*Ephesians 4:30*), quench Him (*1 Thessalonians 5:19*), or in any way rebel against Him (*Isaiah 63:10*). We are setting ourselves up for irrevocable destruction and eternal regret.

My friend, God is very serious about restoring His relationship with you and me. He is not going to stop or give up. We need to get serious about heeding God's call and coming back to Him in true repentance and confession. There is hope, forgiveness, and a glorious future for those who today will say "yes" to God, "yes" to Jesus Christ His Son, and "yes" to the precious Holy Spirit. God's Church needs to offer unrestricted accommodation to the Holy Spirit. He wants to fulfil His divine assignment in our midst.

We have a duty to fulfil in God's process of spiritual restoration and renewal. It is to obey Him at any cost and to make ourselves available to the Holy Spirit. In Scripture, the task of the Holy Spirit is clear: He is the leader of the Church, and we need to give Him full and total access and control. It is time for leaders to step back and afford the Holy Spirit His rightful place in our midst. Only then—when we are willing to do so—will we experience the beginning of true Holy Spirit restoration, renewal and revival in our time.

Apostasy Invokes Abominations

In his vision, Ezekiel—whom I wish to refer to as the Prophet of Revival—witnessed God's people committing terrible abominations as a result of apostasy. In other words, when we backslide, we open the door of our lives to evil forces.

In the vision, recorded in Ezekiel chapter 8, the prophet heard God expressing His utter disgust and abhorrence in no uncertain terms. Ezekiel was sitting in his house with the elders of Judah when God's hand reached out and took him by his hair locks and lifted him up between heaven and earth.

Instantaneously, in the twinkling of an eye, God transported him to Jerusalem, to the door of the northern inner gate of the temple. God was about to show the prophet four disgusting abominations inside the house of God: the image of jealousy; painted images and drawings of idols; women weeping for the idol Tammuz; and His people worshipping the sun. As a result of their apostasy, the leaders had turned to idol worship in God's house.

The first abomination: the image of jealousy

The first abomination was the erection of their idol, the image of jealousy, at the very entrance to the altar in God's house (*Ezekiel 8:5*). God told the prophet that His people had practically evicted Him from His very own sanctuary. The leaders chose to taunt God by erecting this vulgar image in front of God's holy altar. God said to Ezekiel:

> Seest thou what they do? Even the great abominations that the house of Israel committeth here, that I should go far off from my sanctuary?
>
> *Ezekiel 8:6*

God was in effect saying, "Ezekiel, can you believe this? Observe the audacity of my people. They have the nerve to evict me from my own sanctuary!" God was being forcefully evicted and replaced by an idol, right there before His own altar.

The people were coming into the temple to worship this strange idol. They were worshipping an image of jealousy! They knew very well that God was a jealous God, yet they dared to openly taunt and defy Him with such crude and insensitive behaviour.

Something we must understand, my friend, is that when the church backslides and apostasy comes in, the doors will be flung wide open for all kinds of disgusting abominations to take over the sanctuary. So, when God's Holy Spirit gets evicted from the sanctuary, we will most certainly see the entrance of abominations, of which the idol of jealousy will be the forerunner.

The defiant behaviour witnessed by the prophet makes one think of what is happening amongst God's people in our day. The image of jealousy is not something unknown or strange to us. We ought to be familiar with this idol, which is happily worshipped by many of us. When you and I begin to envy other people—their properties, talents or gifts—we are opening ourselves up to the worship of this idol of jealousy.

This idol of jealousy is widely worshipped today, with people trying to outdo one another in their quest to be the best at any cost. Always wanting to come out on top, we end up not caring about the pain, heartache and suffering caused to others by our selfish actions.

God showed the Prophet Ezekiel that this abomination was smack dab in the middle of His holy sanctuary. This is also what is happening today: the idol of jealousy is right in the Church, and God's very own people are bowing to it. My friend, let us be clear about this: apostasy creates, introduces, develops, and encourages abominations in our lives, in our homes, in our churches and in our communities.

The second abomination: paintings of idols

When God showed Ezekiel the first idol, He told him He would go on to show him even more appalling abominations thereafter. God then brought the prophet to a hole in the wall of the sanctuary and told him to dig through it to reach the room on the other side. Ezekiel went into the room and saw paintings and drawings of "every form of creeping things, and abominable beasts, and all the idols of the house of Israel, portrayed upon the wall round about" (*Ezekiel 8:10*).

Then he noticed seventy elders openly practising idolatry in the dark, worshipping the paintings and drawings of idols on the walls. Under the leadership of the Chief Elder Jaazaniah, they were burning incense and paying homage to these painted images. As they engaged in their idolatrous worship, they were saying, "The LORD seeth us not; the LORD hath forsaken the earth" (*Ezekiel 8:12*).

Here were seventy church leaders, under the leadership of their pastor, worshipping idols painted on the walls of the church! These "men of God" were so earnest, serious and desperate in their efforts to taunt and defy God that they went ahead and painted and drew images of their idols on the walls of the church. They were worshipping those images and bowing down before them with burning incense. All of that took place in darkness, while they were chanting, "The Lord does not see, the Lord has forsaken the earth."

They said, "God does not see, He has forsaken the earth." Doesn't this statement sound familiar to you, my friend? When we look at what is happening these days, isn't this what we are seeing? Isn't this what we are saying, through our words, our deeds, our actions, and our interactions with one another, when we do not live in the fear of the Lord? Isn't this what we are saying, when we act as if the Holy Spirit has turned a blind eye to the evil things we do and the way we live?

Think about all the different idols in our lives which we worship. We are in effect saying, "God does not see. God has forsaken the earth."

The Bible, however, declares, "For the eyes of the LORD run to and fro throughout the whole earth, to shew Himself strong in the behalf of them whose heart is perfect toward Him." (*2 Chronicles 16:9*)

Beloved friend, God does indeed see everything we do. He has gone nowhere, nor is He going anywhere. God has not forsaken the earth, for His promise is guaranteed, that He will never leave us nor forsake us. We ought to know that God sees, and that He takes note of everything we do or say!

Idol worship can be very subtle. One needs to take care and be vigilant. Sometimes one can easily become involved in idol worship. The things God has blessed us with may become more important than the God who supplied them in the first place. Think about all the different things in our lives which we may be worshipping, without even realizing they have become our idols!

The third abomination: weeping for Tammuz

After showing Ezekiel the painted idols, God told him that he had not yet seen the worst of the abominations. The prophet was about to see something even more surprising and shocking. God then showed him the women of the church sitting in the courtyard, engaged in idolatrous mourning.

They were weeping and wailing after the foreign idol, Tammuz. They were not shedding tears for their sins or for their families. Nor were they weeping in repentance of their evil ways. No, for some bizarre reason, they were looking north and shedding tears for a strange idol in a foreign land.

They were actually longing to return to Babylon, the land of their captivity, so they could worship Tammuz their idol god. These women were longing to be slaves again in the land of their captivity. How foolish! How demented can one get?

God brought them out of slavery, but they were weeping and mourning to go back into captivity! This is really unbelievable! That was why God told the prophet he would see greater and greater evils, each more shocking than the previous one.

This is a shocking form of apostasy: weeping to be in bondage and captivity, when God has set you free long ago. Wow! But it was not over yet; Ezekiel had not yet seen the ultimate abomination. There was still another abomination God wanted to show him.

The fourth abomination: worshipping the sun

God brought Ezekiel back into the inner court of the temple, between the porch and the altar, and showed him an incredible sight. He saw 25 men—let's say, the executive members of the church board—standing with their backs turned to the temple and their faces facing the east. They were worshipping the sun.

God asked the prophet, "Hast thou seen this, O son of man? Is it a light thing to the house of Judah that they commit the abominations which they commit here?" (*Ezekiel 8:17*) God's people were engaged in idol worship, thinking it was nothing serious; they were just playing around. But for Him, it was a disgusting act—an abomination done to ***provoke Him to anger***.

Therefore will I also **deal in fury**: mine eye shall not spare, **neither will I have pity**: and though they cry in mine ears with a loud voice, yet will I not hear them.

Ezekiel 8:18

These men had turned their backs on God's temple and were facing the east to worship the sun. Worshipping God's creation instead of God the Creator!

God said He would not take it any longer. His people had gone too far and provoked Him to anger! Well, if they wanted to see God angry, then they would have to bear the fury of His holy wrath. If these men did not turn back and repent, they were going to feel God's anger. There would be no pity. Even if they should cry in His ears with a loud voice, God would not hear them.

Wow! My friend, that really is tough. When God in holy anger refuses to hear our cries, then surely we are in very serious trouble!

God responds to the abominations with unrestricted judgment!

Something we need to understand is that, even though God is a God of love, grace and mercy, He simply cannot tolerate sin. Sin of any kind, when honestly confessed to God, will be unconditionally forgiven each and every time. But, when we wilfully continue to defy and taunt God by sinning against Him, then we leave Him with no other option but to come down hard on us in holy wrath and with swift judgment.

This was exactly what happened to the people of God, when they did not repent but continued with the disgusting abominations witnessed by Ezekiel. When we read Ezekiel chapter 9, we find God's patience with His people running out. He had reached the point of irrevocable judgment.

What we see in this whole scenario is a step-by-step progression, leading to the inevitable conclusion of God's judgment. This was the process which brought them to the point of God's divine judgment:

1. Firstly, we witnessed the abomination (*man's defiance of God through idolatry*);
2. Next, the alienation (*God evicted from His sanctuary*);
3. Then, God instituted a process of identification (*the marking of those who repented*);
4. Finally, the conclusion of the whole process (*God's unrestricted judgment and the utter annihilation of the idolaters*).

The process of identification:
those who "cry and sigh"

Ezekiel chapter 9 contains only 11 verses; but, within these few verses, we discover God's express requirements for salvation, renewal and revival. As we read about His firm and swift judgment against those who perpetuate idolatry, we begin to realize just how seriously God views this terrible sin. The first few verses of chapter 9 tell us how God summoned six men carrying weapons of destruction and gave them the command to go into the city of Jerusalem.

Their orders were to "slay utterly" big and small, young and old. God told them, "Do not spare!" and "Have no pity!" (*Ezekiel 9:5-6*) They had been anointed and appointed to execute this awful assignment.

They were instructed to begin their path of destruction at the sanctuary. God's pattern of judgment always starts in His house. We read in *1 Peter 4:17* that "judgment must begin at the house of God".

God decreed, ""First slay the 70 elders!" (*Ezekiel 9:6*) He slayed the elders of the church first, because of their reluctance to deal effectively with their own backslidden condition and that of God's people under their care. God first deals with the leaders of the Church, as the responsibility of apostasy among God's people rests first and foremost with the leadership in the Church.

However, before the destruction began, God called a seventh man and instructed him to go through the city ahead of the six destructors. This seventh man was clothed in white linen, the robe of the High Priest, and he had a writer's inkhorn by his side (*Ezekiel 9:3*). He was told to "set a mark upon the foreheads of [those] that sigh and that cry" for all the abominations practised in the city (*Ezekiel 9:4*).

God says only those who bear His mark, the mark of repentance, will be spared. Only those identified by God as genuinely repentant Christians will be spared. Ezekiel chapter 9 concludes with the man in white linen reporting to God and saying, "I have done as Thou hast commanded me."

The Bible clearly declares in *Hebrews 12:29*, "For our God is a consuming fire"! My friend, God's divine judgment is imminent if we do not turn to Him in genuine repentance. We need to confess our sins, repent, and turn to God with our whole heart, and He certainly will forgive!

We need to hear more messages on repentance coming from our pulpits. Many pastors and leaders have neglected their duty to preach an uncompromised message of repentance. Not only should we encourage and exhort God's people to repent of their sins, but we should also reprove and rebuke the iniquity prevalent in our society.

Whoever does not bear God's mark of forgiveness will have to face the fury of His wrath. No one will be spared. My friend, it is time for us to repent and return to true worship of God in spirit and in truth!

A Vision from God:
Apostasy and Abominations in the Church

Some years ago, when God started dealing with me on the subject of true worshippers, I had a shocking vision one night. In my vision, I was standing in a vast open field where many of my colleagues and acquaintances were gathered for a special occasion.

While everyone was standing around, waiting and talking to one another, I felt I was being drawn away from the crowd, down a slanting embankment to a lower section of this field. I was drawn towards the entrance of what looked like an underground cave.

Standing at the entrance, I could hear music, laughter, and the sound of many voices coming from inside this vast, dimly-lit cave. As I stood at the entrance, listening to the commotion and not knowing what to do next or even what I was doing there, I saw two stark naked young girls walking towards me with big smiles on their faces.

They welcomed me into their "church" and, one on each side of me, took me into this "sanctuary", as they called it. They informed me that I had come at a very special time because they were about to start their initiation service, where new members would be initiated into their church. As we walked through the strange cavern, I realized that sin and evil were very evident in that place. The cave had a strange, nauseating smell. Everywhere I looked, sinful acts were being committed amid shrieks of delight.

I saw people openly engaging in sexual orgies, to shouts of "Hallelujah", "Praise the Lord" and "Glory to God". Others were gathered around gambling tables and, when someone made a win, shouts of "Hallelujah" and "Praise Jesus" were heard from the surrounding crowd. Others were taking part in all kinds of vulgar dancing.

As we moved further through this dark den of sin, I saw people indulging in drinking orgies, swigging down all kinds of alcoholic drinks. Others were snorting cocaine or injecting themselves with all sorts of mainline drugs. While doing this, they were shouting "Praise God" and "Thank you, Jesus".

I also saw people seated in front of huge video screens, watching pornographic movies and openly engaging in all kinds of perverse sexual acts while crying out, "Hallelujah" and "Lord, we praise you".

As we were walking through this sanctuary of evil, I even noticed several pastors and a few familiar faces of well-known men of God. They were all engrossed in some kind of despicable sinful act. I could not believe my eyes. Everything seemed so unreal.

I was witnessing something I had never seen before. It seemed that everything happening in this dark place was supposed to be "worship" offered to Almighty God. I noticed one church elder who recognized me and came over to me to express his pleasure at also seeing me there. He was at one of the gambling tables and was enjoying himself. He was apparently on a winning streak. He turned to me and shouted, "Praise the Lord, Pastor, this is great! Glad to see you're also here!"

I was then escorted to the front section of the sanctuary, where the altar and platform were located. Still on the arms of my two naked escorts, I was brought before a naked woman who was ready to initiate me into their fellowship. She was holding a thin, short, very sharp sword, with which she was about to cut an X into my chest so that blood would flow from the wound. Thus I would enter into a blood covenant with their evil fellowship.

At this point, the power of God came over me. I realized this was a satanic cult, and I could remain silent no longer. I raised my hand and voice and pleaded the blood of Jesus Christ against these demonic forces. I refused to be initiated or cut in any way. I rebuked them in Jesus' name and demanded to be released! They let go of me, and I quickly started making my way toward the exit.

When I finally reached the exit amid the shrieks and shouts of the "worshippers", the Lord had me look back one last time. As I turned around to take one final look at that disgusting scene of "worshippers", the Lord said to me, "My son, I brought you here to give you a glimpse of reality, of what is happening within my Kingdom on earth. What you have seen here *is the condition of my Church today*!"

My dear friend, if what I witnessed in this vision reveals the present condition of God's church, then I am afraid we are in very serious trouble! Something is terribly wrong in the Body of Christ! There is a very urgent need for repentance! We, the leaders of God's church worldwide, need to wake up and return to God.

Praying earnestly about what I had witnessed in this vision, I asked the Lord for clarity and understanding. This is what He showed me. My friend, while we are worshipping, our worship is not directed singularly at Almighty God. Even though we praise and honour Him with our lips, we are in effect openly engaged in idol worship, sinning against God with the lifestyles we have adopted.

God Himself declared in His Word:

Ye hypocrites, well did Esaias prophesy of you, saying, This people draweth nigh unto me with their mouth, and honoureth me with their lips; but their heart is far from me.

Matthew 15:7-8

Wherefore the LORD said, Forasmuch as this people draw near me with their mouth, and with their lips do honour me, but have removed their heart far from me...

Isaiah 29:13

When we continue to engage in things which are abominations to God, we are making a mockery of what is supposed to be true and holy worship to Almighty God. We urgently need to correct whatever has gone wrong with our worship within the Body of Christ internationally.

I was so totally shocked by this disturbing vision. It troubled me for a very long time and still disgusts me to this day. God has given me the responsibility of sharing this vision with you, which is why I am writing this book.

My dear friend, I do believe that apostasy and abominations in God's Church are the serious stumbling blocks to renewal and ultimate revival in our day. These days there seems to be an attitude of "anything goes". The modern mentality is that "there is no need for us to live holy lives before God". We have become manipulators of God's Word, where we interpret Scripture according to our own minds and in a manner that suits our own purposes.

What used to be regarded as wrong and as sin in the past is no longer so regarded. We have become an "enlightened" generation that can very comfortably do without God. We make our decisions based on how we feel and not on what God requires in His holy Word. So, we end up in apostasy, importing abominations into our lives and into our homes, our churches, our communities, and our nations.

We have effectively excommunicated God from our midst, and we carry on as if nothing is wrong. Should we then be at all surprised that our families, our churches, our communities, and our nations around the world are in such dire straits in all aspects of societal existence?

We are fast plunging into an inextricable abyss of irrevocable and irrecoverable moral and social devastation, the extent of which has never been recorded in world history. Is there any hope for us? All I can say is, "Lord, please help us! Please help us to return to you. Help us to repent. Help us, Father, to realize the serious trouble we are in."

My friend, please let us get serious about this issue of true worship. This is not a game. This is for real. I trust that you will now join me as I go in humble prayer before God's Throne of Grace.

As a church leader myself, one convicted in the very depths of my soul by what the Lord has shown me, I now want to pray a prayer of repentance on behalf of myself and all the leaders and members of God's Church worldwide.

If you agree with me, please join me in praying the prayer on the following page.

A Prayer of Repentance

Dear God and Heavenly Father, I come before you in the precious name of Jesus Christ my Saviour. I humbly bow before your holy throne. I am your child, and I love you and serve you as my God. As a leader of people in your divine Kingdom, I want to acknowledge my condition of apostasy, and I confess all of the abominations of idolatry practised in my life over the past years.

I confess that I have sinned wilfully against you by worshipping idols, and that I have, many times in the process, turned my back on you. Heavenly Father, I am very sorry for dishonouring your holy name, and for bringing the ministry you gave me into disrepute.

I am asking that you please forgive me of all my sin and iniquity and that you cleanse me in the precious blood of your Son Jesus Christ. I am now returning to you with all my heart and with all my strength. Today, I rededicate and consecrate my life anew to you and to your service alone.

Lord, I thank you for your forgiveness, and I thank you for giving me another chance. In the precious, marvellous name of Jesus Christ your Son.

Amen.

CHAPTER EIGHT

Fall Down and Worship Me

Jesus tempted by Satan

It is almost unbelievable to learn that even Jesus Christ, the Son of God, was tempted by Satan in the evil one's quest for worship status. One thing we need to realize is that Satan is just as serious as God when it comes to worship. He was evicted from heaven because of his deception, coupled with his desire to be worshipped.

In Matthew chapter 4, we find this significant incident, when Satan tried to con Jesus into worshipping him. This has been Satan's age-old ploy and ambition. He wanted to be God and to have everyone and everything bow before him.

Now, if Satan had no respect for Jesus, the Son of God, what makes us think he will refrain from utilizing the same prowess and deceptive manipulation to get us to worship him? When we study this important portion of Scripture, the first thing that becomes very clear is that we can only conquer Satan by the written Word of God.

Secondly, we discover that this enemy of God knows God's Word. He knows God's Word perfectly. You and I could actually be regarded as amateurs when it comes to the knowledge of God's Word. Satan has been around much longer than we have.

Led of the Spirit

We read in *Matthew 4:1* that Jesus was "led up of the Spirit into the wilderness to be tempted of the devil". Notice that Jesus was specifically **led of the Spirit** for this purpose. It was His Father's will that He be tempted prior to the commencement of His earthly ministry. This was going to be His "trial by fire" in the wilderness. God was serious about having His Son pass the ultimate test, right there in the middle of the wilderness.

It was imperative that our Lord, in the form of man, should gain first-hand experience of temptation. Jesus was going to have to pass this major test all by Himself. No one there but the Holy Spirit. No support from any other person, group, or fellowship of believers. Single and all alone, He was going to have to deal with this challenge, which would be recorded in the annals of human history.

We see something very strange and complex in the developments in this chapter. We may well ask: Why would God's Holy Spirit lead Jesus out into the wilderness specifically "to be tempted of the devil"?

Friend, I have discovered the need for every ministry and ministry gift to go through the purging fire of trial and temptation in order to achieve purity, quality and purpose.

Someone once asked a goldsmith, "When do you know that the gold in the furnace is perfectly purified and completely purged?"

The goldsmith answered, "When I can clearly see the image of my face in the purified gold."

What an amazing revelation! My friend, when you and I find ourselves in the Master's purging fire of trial and temptation, God's desire and main objective is to achieve His divine will and purpose in our lives. In the end, He expects our lives to reflect the image of our Lord and Saviour. Hallelujah!

Jesus' ministry on earth would also begin with Him going through the fires of trial and temptation. Although He was the Son of God, He was also very human. He had the same emotions and weaknesses as any other man. The Bible tells us He fasted forty days and forty nights and then became hungry, like any normal human being. Then came Satan on the scene, when Jesus was hungry, frail and weak.

This is the way the devil operates. He will come when we least expect him. His timing is always spot on. And he utilizes the same method of trickery as he did in the Garden of Eden: launching his attack, ridiculing, and creating doubt in our minds. Let us now study the process of temptation that culminated in Satan's ultimate demand for Jesus to bow down and worship him.

"Turn these stones into bread!"

Satan knew Jesus was hungry, and he certainly also knew that He was the Son of God. So he tempted Him, saying, "If Thou be the Son of God, command that these stones be made bread" (*Matthew 4:3*). But Jesus countered him three times in succession with irrefutable scriptural facts. He declared, "It is written" (*Matthew 4: 4, 7, 10*).

It is written, therefore it is irrefutable. *It is written*, therefore it is unchangeable. *It is written*, therefore it is indelible. *It is written*, therefore it carries an eternal warranty. This warranty never expires. God said it, I believe it, and that settles it!

It is written, "Man shall not live by bread alone, but by every word that proceedeth out of the mouth of God" (*Matthew 4:4*). My friend, you and I *can and shall* live by every word that proceeds from the mouth of our God. It is God's word that gives and sustains life. It is not our marvellous gifts, talents, abilities, professions, treasures or bank balances that keep us alive. We may think so; but please note that, even with all of the above, we will still not survive without God's grace and mercy, and the provision that comes from the Word of God.

We have somehow wilfully or inadvertently neglected to give Almighty God the recognition due to Him for our successes and for the wonderful blessings bestowed daily upon us and our families. We are in fact living and surviving daily on the word that comes from the mouth of God. As the Apostle Paul said with such clarity:

> God that made the world and all things therein... **He giveth to all life, and breath**, and all things... **For in Him we live, and move, and have our being**...
>
> *Acts 17: 24a, 25b, 28a*

Therefore, whether we want to believe it or not, we are in fact living by the word that comes from the mouth of God.

Paul continued to emphasize this truth—that God is our sole Provider—by assuring us in *Philippians 4:19* that "**my God shall supply all your need according to His riches in glory by Christ Jesus**."

So, even though Jesus was hungry after forty days of fasting, and He indeed was able to turn those stones into bread, He was not about to obey Satan in order to satisfy the demands of His physical body. He was in fact living on God's Word and was being sustained by the word that proceeds from the mouth of God His Father. So, Satan lost Round One of the encounter. But, my friend, he did not quit.

Please note: Satan never quits! When he fails the first time, he will come back again and again and again, each time with a new strategy, in the hope of succeeding where he has failed before. *Matthew 4:5* tells us that the devil next transported Jesus out from the wilderness and back into the city of Jerusalem, onto a pinnacle on the roof of the temple... and gave Him Challenge Number Two.

"If Thou be the Son of God, cast Thyself down"

Check out the clever strategy Satan used this time round. He is a master manipulator. He quoted God's word back to God! His strategy was to trick Jesus into obeying him, by misusing the very Word of God that the Son of God was living on.

He started off by demanding, "If Thou be the Son of God, cast Thyself down." Then, to get Jesus to obey him, he quoted *Psalm 91:11-12,* which says, "He shall give His angels charge over thee, to keep thee in all thy ways. They shall bear thee up in their hands, lest thou dash thy foot against a stone."

Observe how he craftily misquoted *Psalm 91:11-12* to try to dupe Jesus into doing his will, when he challenged Him:

> If Thou be the Son of God, cast Thyself down: for it is written, He shall give His angels charge concerning Thee: and in their hands they shall bear Thee up, lest at any time Thou dash Thy foot against a stone.
>
> *Matthew 4:6*

Once again, Jesus responded with the same words, "It is written" but added the word "again". Quoting God's Word from *Deuteronomy 6:16*, Jesus replied, "It is written again, thou shalt not tempt the Lord thy God" (*Matthew 4:7*).

Satan's strategy is still the same today. One of my mentor pastors said, years ago, "If Satan fails to push you down, he will change his strategy and elevate you by pushing you up, if it will achieve his goal. His focus is on achieving his goal, which is to convince us to obey him."

It is very important to understand the response of Jesus in *Matthew 4:7*. He was quoting *Deuteronomy 6:16*, which says, "Ye shall not tempt the LORD your God." Jesus would not accede to Satan's ridiculous demands, just to put God to the test. He always and only does His Father's will.

We need to be careful not to misuse Holy Scripture for our own vain purposes. God will not be manipulated by us. He will not give in to human frivolities and vanities. He is God. He decides by Himself what to do, whether He will do it, and when to do it. When He does respond to our needs and requests, it will be because He has decided on His terms and in His divine wisdom to come to our aid.

Jesus made this fact abundantly clear. God will not be tempted by anyone, even if they were to quote—or, rather, misquote—from the Bible. He is the Boss, He is the Author of the Book. He alone has the power and authority to decide what He will or will not do in any circumstances.

"Fall down and worship me"

Finally, Satan came up with his last challenge. This was actually his eventual goal. This was what he had been working towards from the beginning. He wanted to see Jesus Christ on His face before him, worshipping him. So he took Jesus up to a high mountain and showed Him the kingdoms of the world and the glory of them. Then he said to Jesus, "All these things will I give Thee, if Thou wilt fall down and worship me" (*Matthew 4:9*).

Let us take a closer look at this final scene. Jesus was taken to a very high mountain and shown the kingdoms of this world and the glory of them. Then Satan offered Him "all these things" if He would fall down and worship him.

Friends, we need to remind ourselves that the Psalmist David declared, "The earth is the LORD's, and the fullness thereof; the world, and they that dwell therein" (*Psalm 24:1*). Now, I am wondering what it was that Satan was promising to give to Jesus, should He bow down and worship him?

If the earth is the Lord's, and the fullness thereof, including everyone who dwells on the earth, then what is it that Satan could really offer Jesus? In fact, we need to ask the question, "What does Satan own?"

Does he own the earth? The answer is no!

Does he own the world? The answer is no! Does he own the peoples and the nations of the earth? The answer is no! Does he own hell? The answer is still an emphatic no! Because even hell was created by God and prepared for the devil and his angels (*Matthew 25:41*).

Does he own the soul of any person? The answer is no! God's Word declares, "Behold, all souls are mine; as the soul of the father, so also the soul of the son is mine: the soul that sinneth, it shall die" (*Ezekiel 18:4*).

So, my friend, is there anything that belongs to the devil which he could offer Jesus Christ? The answer is still no! Satan has been a liar and a deceiver from the beginning. He cannot speak the truth. He has nothing to offer us; yet billions are willing to follow and worship him.

Over many centuries, people throughout the world have been duped and deceived by the false promises of this evil one. Many millions will realize too late that they have been deceived. There will be no chance to turn back, and it will be too late to rectify the mistakes they have made in life.

"Worship the Lord thy God"

God's message is loud and clear, His response firm and unambiguous. Jesus gave Satan His final answer, declaring in no uncertain terms, "Thou shalt worship the Lord thy God, and **Him only** shalt thou serve" (*Matthew 4:10b*). Jesus made it clear that His emphasis was on "HIM ONLY": God is the only one we should worship and serve.

Satan's age-long ambition has been for us to fall down and idolize him; to offer him the worship that in truth does not belong to him. But Jesus Christ settled the issue forever: all God's creatures will serve and worship only God the Father. There is no room for worship of any god other than the only living, true and wise God.

The very first commandment God gave Moses way back then is still in force: "Thou shalt have no other gods before me" (*Exodus 20:3*). Almighty God alone is to be worshipped.

Satan has been a liar, cheater and deceiver from the very beginning. He is a master manipulator who will use Scripture to manipulate and deceive us. He will attack us when we are at our weakest. Be assured, my friend, he never gives up. He will try again and again to achieve his goal. Jesus gained first-hand experience of his method of operation, but He knew how to deal with the evil one.

When Satan quoted Scripture, Jesus quoted Scripture back at him. Jesus made Satan understand exactly who was in charge! God was in charge, and He was calling the shots. Hallelujah! God was not about to relinquish His authority and abdicate His throne, simply because of Satan's deception. No way! God is God and will remain as God throughout all eternity. He will be worshipped by His Creatures of Worship throughout time and eternity!

We Do Not Remain in the Wilderness

Friend, one wonderful thing about going through the "wilderness experience" of trials, temptations, tribulations and hardships is that we do not remain there for the rest of our lives. It comes but for a season. For His purposes, God leads me into the wilderness—and through the wilderness!

When I have passed my test, and my gold is purified and purged, the same Holy Spirit who led me into the wilderness will lead me out into glorious victory! Into new ministry, new anointing, new possibilities, new exploits, new breakthroughs!

While I am in the wilderness, the situation may become unbearable. I may very well reach the point of wanting to quit. But this is all part and parcel of the refining process. You see, my friend, the Promised Land lies beyond the wilderness! My victory awaits me on the other side of the wilderness. This is a journey I have to take in order to reach that glorious Promised Land of victory, power and anointing.

The main thing we must remember is this: do not remain in the wilderness! When the battle is over and the victory is won, move on out of the wilderness into the Promised Land! Claim and take the victory which is yours in Jesus' Name!

Do not remain in the wilderness after you have passed the test! Great, mighty and supernatural exploits are now beckoning on the horizon. They are saying "Come on out!"

Come out into the Promised Land of supernatural glory, grace and power. Affluence and prosperity are yours for the taking! Come on out! Move on forward! Now, just trust God for the victory! Do it in Jesus' Name! Hallelujah!

CHAPTER NINE

The Prophet of Worship and Revival

A look at the Prophet Ezekiel's ministry

In this chapter, we want to make a brief study of the book of Ezekiel. We are trusting the Holy Spirit for divine illumination and revelation, as examine the developments described by this marvellous man of God. Here we are witnessing a prophet of worship and revival.

This prophet was used of God in a most dynamic manner, specifically to proclaim and expose the sins of God's people. To him was given an assignment for which very few servants of God in our day would qualify. It was a divine assignment that required the highest degree of integrity. It was a ministry of zero compromise.

God personally qualified the prophet for this specific job. First of all, the name Ezekiel means "God makes me strong" or "The Lord strengthens me". What a name! I believe God gave him this name for a very good reason. This was the same prophet to whom He gave a forehead as hard as a diamond!

The messages given to Ezekiel to deliver to God's people were tough and hard. But God made him strong, and He encouraged him to speak up boldly and not to fear intimidation from the people. Ezekiel was God's faithful servant, appointed and significantly used of God to warn, reprimand and rebuke His people.

As a predominant worship and revival prophet, Ezekiel was given the closest look at God's heavenly operations. Few other prophets have seen such divine mysteries. For instance, Isaiah, Daniel, and John the Revelator were each given the opportunity to witness end-time events. But to Ezekiel alone was shown the most impressive exhibition of God's power in action; he was privileged to witness the birth of God's Church, born in the holy fire of Pentecost.

So now, let us turn to the Book of Ezekiel, to see what more God wants to teach us through this excellent Prophet of Revival. We will certainly gain greater clarity and a better understanding of true worship, as we study the prophet's message. For many, Ezekiel is a closed book, difficult to understand; but, when we take time to ask the Holy Spirit for illumination and insight, God will reveal to us the glory and wonder in this book.

We want to make an in-depth study of what the prophet saw and heard in his visions. As previously mentioned, there is amazing power in the glorious imagery and symbolism within this book. We need only to take the time and walk calmly through Ezekiel's visions to begin to experience the dynamic power of God, available to us right here, right now. Ezekiel was God's strong Prophet; God made him strong for the ministry he was called to perform.

Ezekiel was a man with the ability to "tell it like it is". When we meet him for the first time, we see someone in a very difficult situation: "I was among the captives by the river of Chebar" (*Ezekiel 1:1*).

114

We find this man of God in a place where most of us would be discouraged, stressed and depressed. But not so with Ezekiel. Here was a man held in bondage in Babylon with the rest of God's people. But notice his attitude, even while in captivity in a strange land. He did not allow his condition or his circumstances to limit him in the ministry to which God had called him. Even though he was in captivity, he was still God's prophet and was available for service. The chains, the restrictions, the scrutiny of the guards watching him, and all the other negative forces working against him did not weaken his resolve. Though bound, Ezekiel was absolutely free in the spirit.

Listen to his report:

> Now it came to pass... as I was among the captives by the river of Chebar, that the heavens were opened, and I saw visions of God.
>
> *Ezekiel 1:1*

Ezekiel's experience tells us that there is no man-made obstacle able to either block, stifle or hinder the Spirit of God from operating in our lives. God's divine will *must and will* break through, if we are available. Even in exile, in prison among captives, on land or sea or in the air, God's Holy Spirit cannot be restricted by any earthly force.

This is what Ezekiel said, in effect: "When I was in captivity, bound and restricted by man, THEN the heavens were opened, and I saw visions of God! Hallelujah! It was when I was in a no-win situation, when I felt lost and rejected, that was when God came through for me!"

What an awesome God we serve! Please believe this, my friend. God excels in adverse situations. He specializes in hopeless cases. He is a champion when it comes to things thought impossible! When the odds are stacked against us: that is when He exhibits His miraculous power! Hallelujah!

Right now, may I ask you, what is it which is binding you today? What is keeping you captive and imprisoned? What is holding you back, so much so that God's will cannot be accomplished in your life? You can be freed right now, my friend—because the same power and anointing which rested on Ezekiel is now resting on you and me. You can be totally free right now, in Jesus' name!

Do not focus on your circumstances. Do not succumb to those negative thoughts, those feelings of discouragement, stress and depression. God's power is setting you free right now! Take it! Be free, in Jesus' name! Be delivered, in Jesus' name! Be loosed, in Jesus' name! Amen and Amen!

Do you feel the presence of God? He is here right now! Now, thank Him and praise Him for deliverance, liberty and freedom! God is giving you the victory!

Out of the Midst of the Fire

Ezekiel saw Creatures of Worship coming forth out of the fire. It was like they were created or born in the fire:

> And I looked, and, behold, a whirlwind came out of the north, a great cloud, and a fire infolding itself, and a brightness was about it, and out of the midst thereof as the colour of amber, out of the midst of the fire.

116

Also out of the midst thereof came the likeness of four living creatures. And this was their appearance; they had the likeness of a man.

Ezekiel 1:4-5

Those Creatures of Worship moved and operated by fire. Fire was an integral part of their existence. It seemed that they were activated by the power generated by the fire. Friend, we read in the book of Acts that the Church of Jesus Christ was born and created in the holy fire of Pentecost. God created for Himself a true Creature of Worship when He sent down flaming tongues of fire from heaven:

And there appeared unto them **cloven tongues like as of fire**, and it sat upon each of them. And they were all **filled with the Holy Ghost**, and began to speak with other tongues, as the Spirit gave them utterance.

Acts 2:3-4

John the Baptist, the forerunner of Jesus, declared one day to his disciples:

I indeed baptize you with water unto repentance. But He that cometh after me is mightier than I, whose shoes I am not worthy to bear: He shall baptize you **with the Holy Ghost and with FIRE!**"

Matthew 3:11

This marvellous Creature of Worship, the true Church of Jesus Christ, was born in the fire! It came forth out of the midst of the fire—the fire of the Holy Spirit!

117

We have already dealt with some of the Seraphim's features in Chapters Five and Six. But now Ezekiel tells us more about their appearance, as he watched them coming from the midst of the fire. A strong, bright light emanated from them, like a powerful lamp illuminating its environment and dispelling the darkness. This was how the prophet described them:

> Their appearance was like burning coals of fire, and like the appearance of lamps: it went up and down among the living creatures; and the fire was bright, and out of the fire went forth lightning.
>
> *Ezekiel 1:13*

Fire and light are important characteristics of God and of the heavenly realm. God is love and God is light. He is a God of love, but He is also "a consuming fire" (*Hebrews 12:29*). Jesus confirmed this when He declared:

> I am the light of the world: he that followeth me shall not walk in darkness, but shall have the light of life.
>
> *John 8:12*

Then He did something marvellous: He transferred this glorious light to His disciples when He declared, "Ye are the light of the world" (*Matthew 5:14*).

God's Creature of Worship, His church, born and created in fire, operates by the fire of the Holy Spirit. The church, designed to emanate the glorious light of Jesus Christ into a dark and dying world, now truly ought to be the light of the world, as instructed by our Lord.

They Were Controlled by the Spirit of God

Ezekiel noticed one outstanding feature of these marvellous Creatures of Worship: they were totally under the control of God's Holy Spirit.

> And they went every one straight forward: whither the Spirit was to go, they went; and they turned not when they went.
>
> *Ezekiel 1:12*

They were subject to the leading and the inspiration of the Spirit. Sounds familiar, does it not? They went straight forward, and they turned not when they went. They followed strictly the leading of the Spirit. They followed only one route. They only went straight forward, following after the Holy Spirit.

God's Creatures of Worship move in response to the Spirit of God. Ezekiel emphasized the fact that, wherever the Spirit went, they followed. They were inspired and energized by the movement of the Spirit. The Church would do well to take note of this very important truth.

Let us give the Spirit of God His rightful position in the Church. Let us afford Him freedom and liberty to do His job, which is to lead, guide and convict us. Jesus assured us that "when He, the Spirit of truth, is come, He will guide you into all truth..." (*John 16:13*) I do believe we will once again see the Church in all of its glory, just like in the book of Acts, when we totally submit to the leadership of the Holy Spirit in our midst.

The Holy Spirit has been given an assignment by God the Father. It is His job to lead, to teach, and to convict us, and to bring to remembrance whatever has been declared by Jesus Christ. We would do well to open the doors of our hearts, our churches, our congregations, our organizations, our denominations, our boards, our committees, our homes, and our lives to Him, and allow Him free rein.

I also believe God wants to restore His church to its full potential and power, and to bring us back to our original status, like it was on the day of Pentecost. There was Power. There was Authority. There was Vision. There was Integrity. There was Genuine Spirituality. The gifts and ministries were all fully operative under the leadership of the Holy Spirit. No place for lies and deceit. No place for corruption. No place for cheating. No place for wilful sin. There was order in the church, and it was God's order with no compromise. It was a matter of obedience and submission to God's will at all times. Man was not in control of God's Church. God the Holy Spirit was in charge at all times.

This is what the Church needs today. We need to return to God-ordained leadership. We need to surrender and hand over the leadership of the Church to the Holy Spirit! I believe, when we do this, we will begin to witness a mighty breakthrough in our midst, the like of which we have never seen before. The church will once again BE THE CHURCH!

Ezekiel, in describing the dazzling movements of these Creatures of Worship, reported that they "ran and returned as the appearance of a flash of lightning" (*Ezekiel 1:14*).

These wonderful creatures were endowed with the speed of lightning. They moved faster than fast—like a "flash of lightning"! Wow! That's fast! These are no sluggish or lazy creatures. They can move at super speed. One could almost call them mean machines! Fast and effective!

The Great Commission assigned to the Church by our Lord Jesus is a task to be executed with speed, for we have only a fixed amount of time to accomplish it. Our methods need to be fast and effective. The Creature needs to act swiftly in its execution of this assignment. There is no time to waste, no time to sit idly and relax, while millions of souls are dying daily without knowing Jesus as their Saviour.

The Creature has been empowered with lightning speed to deliver the message. Lightning speed by way of air travel, radio, television, the internet and cell phones. The message must be relayed and proclaimed quickly and effectively. Yes, we have been endowed with speed to fulfil our assignment. Whatever we wish to do for the cause of Christ we need to do fast; and we need to do it now, today, this hour, this moment. Now is the time to get up and GO in Jesus' name!

A Wheel in the Middle of a Wheel

In *Ezekiel 1:16*, the prophet described another strange and significant development: "The appearance of the wheels and their work... was as it were a wheel in the middle of a wheel." Ezekiel saw a massively huge wheel, in the middle of which appeared to be another wheel moving in sync with it. In describing the enormous size of the huge wheel, he said it was so high that it was "dreadful" (*Ezekiel 1:18*).

Now comes the action. He saw that, when the living creatures moved, the wheels moved with them. When they ascended or went up, the wheels went up. When they descended, the wheels also descended. The wheels moved in sync with them. The two were strangely connected to one another in their movement and action. It seemed to be a joint movement. The one was part of the other.

Let us now ponder upon this marvellous scene. The movement of the huge and "dreadful" wheel was the force of power. I believe this huge and dreadful wheel represents the awesome presence of God. In the middle of this wheel was another wheel, representing the power of God and His Spirit, which generates and creates life and movement.

The movement of the wheel in the middle of a wheel is the power of the Holy Spirit moving within the centre of the parameters created by Almighty God. They move in unity as one force. The power of God energizes the living creatures in their assignments. The wheels move in tandem with them. Whichever direction the Spirit leads, they move; and the wheels move with them.

The Prophet also noticed lots of eyes all around the circumference of the huge wheel. These eyes represent the omnipotence and omnipresence of God. His eyes see everything. He notices each and every action we take and every move we make. As it says in *Proverbs 15:3,* "The eyes of the LORD are in every place, beholding the evil and the good." He moves with us everywhere we go. He is always with us, and He is all around us, to act mightily on our behalf.

The eyes of the LORD run to and fro throughout the whole earth, to shew Himself strong in the behalf of them whose heart is perfect toward Him.

2 Chronicles 16:9

So, the huge wheel in the middle of the enormous wheel must surely represent the awesome power of God, whose eyes are constantly on each and every movement of His creatures. His mighty power energizes the living creatures to execute His will and to move by the power of the Holy Spirit resident within the very centre of His purpose.

God's ultimate modus operandi regarding these living creatures is for them to move and perform in accordance with His will and power. He empowers them, He leads them, and He totally controls them.

Remember what Jesus said? He told us that without Him we can do nothing! And that is so true. It's a fact. My friend, you and I can do nothing without Him. He is our only source of existence and sustenance.

The Round Design of the Wheel
(God's mark throughout Creation)

The circular shape of the wheel that Ezekiel saw is truly significant. God Himself is the designer of the wheel. He invented the round form, not only of the wheel, but of everything that is circular throughout all of creation. The design of the circle is evident everywhere throughout the whole universe. One can actually identify the circle as God's mark throughout creation.

This discovery was amazing because, the more I looked at creation, the more I saw the mark of the circle everywhere. First of all, the cell is round. When we look at a human cell under a microscope, the overall appearance will be the form of a circle. The human body is made up of many billions of cells. Indeed, most earthly matter consists of billions of cells pressed together. The blood flowing through the various organs in the human body consists of billions of cells. These billions of blood cells are keeping us alive day after day.

A nucleus is circular. So is an embryo within the womb of its mother. All our veins, arteries and capillaries, through which our blood travels through our bodies, are circular tubes. The eyeball, the iris, and the pupil in our eyes are all circular. Our eardrums are circular. A strand of hair is a thin circular tube. The marks of our fingerprints are all circular.

Most seeds of plants, trees and flowers are circular. A grain of sand, the crest of a wave, a droplet of water, and the age circles on a tree trunk: they are all circular. The earth, the planets, the sun, the moon, the stars, and the shapes of galaxies are all circular. Cloud formations, winds, tornadoes and hurricanes all move in circular motions. Drop a stone into a pool of water or smash a rock into the earth, and you will see a circle. The shape of the rainbow is also circular, although we get to see only the top half of it.

All these things bear the design of God's mark, the circle. No beginning and no ending. That is why the ring is a significant symbol of love and devotion. It bears God's mark, for God is love.

I believe the wheel, circular in shape, is God's mark throughout His creation. It is the symbol of completeness and perfection! No shortcomings. Full and complete. Perfect. We use terms like "a new wave of revival" or "a new wave of God's glory", and we are right to do so. The crest of the wave bears God's mark of the circle.

The huge wheel of God's presence is in operation right now, all across the universe. And the wheel in the middle of this wheel is feverishly in operation, as God's Holy Spirit moves in for the final and greatest revival this world has ever witnessed.

We, God's people, need to position ourselves for the last and final wave that is about to hit the earth in all of its glory! Friends, get ready! It's coming soon! It could even happen this very day! Hallelujah! These are the last days, and God promised it would happen in these last and final days! This world is ready for a divine visitation from heaven!

The Glory of the Lord

What the prophet saw next in his vision was a most wonderful scene, which he recorded in *Ezekiel 1:22-28*. He was about to behold the very throne of God, surrounded by the glory of God—with astounding consequences. He first of all observed what he called a "firmament" over the heads of the creatures. The firmament was a heavenly expanse up above them, filled with glory, fire and light, and with an atmosphere of divine holiness.

Then Ezekiel heard the sound of their wings when they moved. It was like the sound of great waters and like the voice of the Almighty. It was like the voice of speech. It was like the voice of God speaking. He next saw, elevated in the air over the heads of the creatures, the likeness of a throne glistening like a sapphire stone.

Ezekiel then witnessed the likeness of a man sitting upon this glorious throne of shimmering sapphire. He described the appearance of the one who sat on the throne as like "the appearance of fire". It seemed as if He was engulfed by the fire, but He was not consumed by it. Then there appeared what looked like a rainbow encircling the throne. Finally the prophet came face to face with Almighty God:

> This was the appearance of the likeness of the glory of the LORD. And when I saw it, I fell upon my face, and I heard a voice of one that spake.
>
> *Ezekiel 1:28(b)*

We were earlier introduced to the prophet's vision, which now culminates in his appearance before God's holy throne. When the prophet experienced the awesome glory of God, he fell upon his face. Then God said to him, "Son of man, stand upon thy feet, and I will speak unto thee." The Spirit entered into him and lifted him to his feet. And God spoke to him:

> Son of man, I send thee to the children of Israel, **to a rebellious nation that hath rebelled against me: they and their fathers have transgressed against me, even unto this very day.**
>
> *Ezekiel 2:3*

Listen to God's introductory message: "I am sending you to my people, the children of Israel, a rebellious nation that has rebelled against me even to this very day." Wow! What an assignment! The prophet was expressly chosen by God to go and preach a message of repentance to a nation which had turned rebellious against Almighty God!

Here was God's holy nation, His own people, rebelling against Him since the time of their fathers, even to that very day! Isn't it sad when a people backslide and turn their backs on God in rebellion? And for generations afterwards, to their own detriment, they refuse to repent and return to Him?

But, do you know what? We live in times when exactly the same thing is happening. Many nations throughout the world have for generations done exactly the same thing. They have forsaken the only true and living God and have rebelled against Him by turning to idol worship.

It has happened even in our western, so-called "Christian" countries. We have decided we do not need God anymore. We can get by on our own. We have now become too civilized to the extent that we do not need God anymore. We have even increased our knowledge and have become rich by multiplying our hoarded resources (*Revelation 3:17*).

We arrogantly believe we can do everything ourselves, so we have expelled God from our vocabulary— except when we use His name in vain. God has been expelled from our homes, our schools, our institutions of higher learning, and even from our halls of government and houses of parliament. We have decided to rebel against God! We have taken upon ourselves to ignore Him and His Holy Spirit.

God has even been expelled from the doors of many of our so-called "churches". We have decided to break God's laws and statutes. We have established for ourselves our own "man-made godless society", in which GOD has no part. Surely we are rebelling against God. Our communities, our nations, and our governments are rebelling against Almighty God. Even our churches are rebelling against Almighty God.

Church leaders and pastors are rebelling against Almighty God. We dare to continue to ignore Him, ignore His precious Holy Spirit, and indulge in all kinds of man-made fleshly ceremonies and rituals, in which God has no part to play. We have appointed fleshly, carnally-minded men and women to our boards and committees to rule our churches. People who have no spiritual insight or any idea of what is important to Almighty God. Many of them do not know or care about any of God's priorities. Decisions are made which negatively affect God's Church, and inhibit, stifle and block God's plans and purposes. In this manner, many are in rebellion against Almighty God. This present condition of apostasy in God's Church has become a worldwide phenomenon.

The Holy Spirit has been expelled from our churches. He has no chance to come in and lead and teach the Church in the manner ordained by Almighty God. It is time that God's holy prophets stand up upon their feet and prophesy. In these last and final days, they need to declare God's word to the Church and to the nations of this world. God is urgently calling us all to repentance.

Listen to how God further described His people: "they are impudent children and stiff hearted" (*Ezekiel 2:4a*). God then told Ezekiel, "I do send thee unto them; and thou shalt say unto them, Thus saith the Lord GOD" (*Ezekiel 2:4b*).

Throughout most of Ezekiel's prophetic ministry, God clearly specified the terminology he should use in his proclamations. He was to prophesy to them, "Thus saith the Lord God."

The prophetic ministry of this true man of God could actually be identified by two specific phrases which were repeated over and over again. They are "Thus saith the Lord God" and "they shall know that I am God".

This man truly was God's Servant. He was God's appointed mouthpiece, and he did not let fear of the people hold him back from proclaiming God's word to them. At the start, when God called him into ministry, he had felt fear and apprehension. But God assured him that He would be with him to support him; thus he should not be afraid of the people.

The fear of people is possibly one of the most common faults in the lives of Servants of God today. We seem to forget so easily who it was who has called us into ministry. Our allegiance and loyalty to God seem to become difficult issues at times when we need to choose between God and man. When we hear from God, and He instructs us to convey His word to His people, we tend to freeze and fear the reaction of people to the message. But the fact remains, it is not our word, it is the word of Almighty God!

Ezekiel declared, "Thus saith the Lord God!" God said it; and I, as His servant, must simply proclaim it! All of God's servants daily face this major challenge: either to obey God and proclaim His unadulterated holy word, or to bow to the fear of people and keep quiet. But the genuinely called, anointed and appointed Servant of God knows where he or she stands on this important issue.

These Servants of God have the faith and courage to stand up for the truth in the face of opposition, hostility, scorn, ridicule and persecution. These are God's True Champions! These are the men and women who, over the centuries, have formed the very foundation of the Christian faith. Just like the Prophet Ezekiel, they were totally sold out to God and His divine will and purpose. Nothing else mattered in their earthly existence except to simply obey and please Almighty God. These were truly God's servants who were able to proclaim fearlessly, "Thus saith the Lord God!"

Friends, if ever there was a time this world needs to hear from God, that time is now! We need to hear from God! The message must be crystal clear and without compromise! A message of repentance, salvation, deliverance.

A message of hope for the hopeless. A message of healing for the diseased and the afflicted. A message of peace for those involved in endless wars that no one wins. A message of good news in a world where bad news is all that people hear. A message which unashamedly proclaims, loud and clear around the world: "Jesus Christ is still the answer for the world today!"

Please note, Jesus Christ is not "one of the answers" to this world's chaos and calamity. No. He is THE ONLY ANSWER. We have tried everything possible to address the major problems we are facing, but to no avail. Nations are still fighting. Wars are still raging around the globe. Nation fighting against nation, tragedies and calamities occurring daily. Millions dying of HIV, Aids and other diseases never heard of before.

Babies are having babies, as a result of the decay in moral standards throughout the world. Prisons everywhere are over-populated. Young boys and girls are behind bars because of a lack of order and discipline in their homes and communities. They learn about the "facts of life" on the streets, because there is no one to teach them the right way. Marriages and families are disintegrating right before our eyes. Governments with no genuine, upright or righteous leaders, with corruption and bribery being the order of the day.

No one has any solution to the horrible state of affairs throughout this world. That is why the Church needs to unashamedly proclaim the name of Jesus Christ. Jesus alone is THE ANSWER. Let us declare it. Let us proclaim it in the media, on the radio, on television, and on any other form of worldwide communication. Broadcast this message loud and clear, everywhere! Jesus Christ is the one and only answer for the world today!

CHAPTER TEN

David, a Man after God's Own Heart

A role model of a true worshipper

We are about to make some significant discoveries as we study David's life story. Here is an exceptional Servant of God, one who was personally commended by God Himself as "a man after mine own heart" (*Acts 13:22*).

When the Holy Spirit initially instructed me to write this book, I felt hopelessly ignorant and seriously inadequate to assume this assignment, which to my mind was beyond my own personal abilities. But then the Lord took me on a journey through the life of this man of God, and I discovered the secret of David's success. I discovered the simplicity and genuine sincerity which governed his life and which have impacted countless lives over many centuries.

Without a doubt, David was a true worshipper. One only needs to read his Psalms to understand the really close relationship he had with Father God. From the moment he inadvertently stepped onto the scene, when Samuel came to Jesse's house to anoint a new king for Israel, we notice this special young man.

God's favour rested upon David; and when the Prophet Samuel anointed him as king, "the Spirit of the Lord came upon David from that day forward" (*1 Samuel 16:13*).

However, in the very next verse, we read the opposite about Saul: "the Spirit of the LORD departed from Saul, and an evil spirit from the LORD troubled him" (*1 Samuel 16:14*). How devastating it is, when the Spirit of God departs from one's life! For Saul, life must have become an awful and empty existence without the precious Holy Spirit to lead and guide him. But then, my friend, this is what happens to us when we become disobedient to Almighty God.

In David, we find the direct opposite. God endorsed him as a man after His own heart. I became curious about this young man. I wanted to discover what it was that qualified him for such favour with God. What did David have and what did he do that caught God's attention? This young man impressed Almighty God! What an achievement, to be able to impress Almighty God!

Well, my friend, when I started closely studying the life of David, I made a few really astonishing discoveries. These I now wish to share with you. They certainly form the very foundation of the life of a true worshipper.

David Trusted Almighty God Absolutely

I believe that David was so highly favoured by God because, from a young age, he had developed and exercised an absolute, unquestioning faith in Almighty God. Here was a young boy out in the field, tending his father's sheep and doing his job with genuine commitment. David had an easy-going, nonchalant attitude as he watched over the sheep placed in his care by his father Jesse.

Psalm 23 was born out of his shepherding experiences, as he dealt with the challenges and dangers that shepherds face daily. I also believe David used those hours of quiet solitude in the field to stay in touch with his God. When we read *Psalm 23*, it becomes clear to us that David developed a very special relationship with God over those lonely years as he shepherded the sheep.

One day his father Jesse called him home and sent him to the battlefield with a lunch basket for his brothers, who were fighting in King Saul's army (*1 Samuel 17:17-18*). At the same time that he arrived on the scene, the Philistine giant Goliath had just stepped out to challenge and taunt Saul and his men once more. Goliath was calling for a man from the Israeli army to come forth and fight with him.

All the men in Saul's army fled and hid from this huge Philistine. No one had the courage to step forward to face the challenge. The attitude of fear and apprehension displayed by his countrymen deeply disappointed the young man. There was no one in the camp willing to trust the God of Israel. No one except this young boy David, who had absolute faith in his Almighty God.

In fact, he requested to be brought before King Saul and, when he was brought before the king, he offered to go out and fight Goliath. He presented the king with his testimony of how God had enabled him to kill the lion and the bear which were threatening his flock. He then declared that this same God would give him victory over Goliath.

David knew the secret of success and victory, and he was trying to share it with King Saul and his army. They were all shocked by the size of Goliath and feared him. However, in their fear, they failed to recognize and acknowledge the greatness and power of their God. They saw their problem as bigger than their God.

David simply did the opposite. He recognized and proclaimed the greatness and power of his God, and the insignificance of this giant whom everyone feared. He proclaimed that his God was greater than the problem they were facing. This young man had absolute faith in his God. In faith, he actually declared victory before he even stepped up to face the giant. He announced to Goliath:

> I come to thee in the name of the LORD of hosts, the God of the armies of Israel, whom thou hast defied. This day will the LORD deliver thee into mine hand!
>
> *1 Samuel 17:45b-46a*

Well, as they say, the rest is history. David defeated Goliath with one tiny pebble propelled into the giant's forehead by the power of God Almighty. David practised blind faith in his God and was victorious every time. This seemingly simple, nonchalant, down-to-earth young boy made world history by killing a giant—with only a sling and a pebble as weapons!

I believe God singled David out as a man after His own heart because of the blind faith he placed in Him. He trusted God all the way, whatever the cost. Here was a man who was totally sold out to God.

David's relationship with his God was his top priority. His life was the most tangible and perfect example of what we may call a "lifestyle of worship". He lived to worship God continuously and to the uttermost. It was not only a priority but also a pleasure for him to serve God in spirit and in truth.

David Knew How to Pray

My second discovery concerns David's prayer life. This man knew how to pray and communicate with God. Prayer was a very important part of his life, and he prayed at least three times a day. He declared in *Psalm 55:17*, "Evening, and morning, and at noon, will I pray, and cry aloud: and He shall hear my voice."

David combined his prayer life with constant fasting, as he revealed in *Psalm 109:24*: "My knees are weak through fasting; and my flesh faileth of fatness." It is clear that David practised regular prayer and fasting. Any person with a desire to maintain a healthy relationship with God would do well to take note of the example shown by this true worshipper. David's prayer life mirrored that of our Lord and Saviour Jesus Christ.

We have to maintain a healthy prayer life if we are to be successful worshippers. Almighty God desires our daily communication with Him. In fact, when Jesus walked the earth, He was in continuous communication with His Father day and night. As our primary role model of the True Worshipper, Jesus exemplifies for us the importance of continuous communication with the Father through prayer.

David did exactly the same. He prayed three times a day and fasted regularly. This should inspire us to dedicate ourselves to a more committed prayer life, which is essential if we want to be true worshippers of God. I believe it is also the first step towards becoming a man or woman after God's own heart.

How many times a day do we pray? David has set us a good example. Here was a man after God's heart because he knew how to pray. He knew what was important for maintaining a healthy relationship with God. He let nothing interfere with his time alone with God, three times a day.

David Knew How to Praise

Thirdly, I believe David qualified as a man after God's own heart because he knew how to praise God. He knew how to praise with no holds barred! Nothing stopped this man from praising his God! He was the first worshipper who did not allow anyone or anything to inhibit him in his praise of God.

He declared in *Psalm 119:164*, "Seven times a day do I praise Thee because of Thy righteous judgments." The man dedicated seven specific, appointed times a day just to praise Almighty God. Wow! What dedication! What discipline! When David started praising God, he did it well indeed!

He proclaimed in *Psalm 103:1*, "Bless the LORD, O my soul: and all that is within me, bless His holy name!" David praised God with everything that was within him—with total, exuberant, uninhibited praise. I believe this is the way God wants to be praised. The Bible teaches us that God inhabits the praises of His people (*Psalm 22:3*).

138

God truly enjoys our praise! When we praise God, we should do it properly, just as David did. We should do it exuberantly and without any reservation! Everything within us should combine in the act of praise we offer to God. He alone is worthy of all of our praise and adoration!

Constant and continuous praise is the way David did it. He did it seven times a day and he did it well, and God enjoyed and inhabited his praises! This man knew how to praise! Praise is synonymous with the Psalmist David.

God could depend on this young man when it came to fulsome, fervent and total praise! David brought the book of Psalms to an exhilarating conclusion when he exclaimed in the last verse of the last Psalm, "Let everything that hath breath praise the LORD. Praise ye the LORD!" (*Psalm 150:6*)

My friend, how many times a day do we praise God? Once? Twice? Or never? Once again, you and I can learn much from the life of this true worshipper. I believe his method and mode of praise must surely have impressed God. When God expressed His approval of this young man, He called him a man after His own heart—because David knew how to praise Him.

David Knew How to Worship

The fourth discovery I made was that God called David a man after His own heart because he knew how to worship. The true quality of this worshipper comes through in many of his Psalms, as he sang of the power and glory of God, while acknowledging his own fallibilities and inadequacies.

Listen to his call to worship:

O come, let us worship and bow down: let us kneel before the LORD our maker. For He is our God; and we are the people of His pasture, and the sheep of His hand.

Psalm 95:6-7

Falling down prostrate in the presence of our holy God was normal practice for this true worshipper. Humbling himself in the dust of the earth seemed to be no hard thing for this man after God's own heart.

In *Psalm 132:7* David declared, "We will go into His tabernacles, we will worship at His footstool." You see, my friend, when we fully realize and recognize the awesome greatness of Almighty God in the manner that David did, worshipping on our faces in God's holy presence becomes an obligatory practice.

Many times, as I watch people of the Islamic faith in worship, I realize all the more keenly the inadequacy of Christian worship. These people go down on their knees and fall down on their faces as they pray. This seems to be the manner of worship exemplified by David. Not only down on his knees, but down on his face before God.

For the true worshipper, falling down on one's face in God's holy presence is an honour. David knew how to worship, down on his face, prostrate at the footstool of the Lord. I believe God was impressed by David's humility and by his genuine heart for true worship. Therefore God personally qualified him as a man after His own heart.

David Knew How to Confess and Repent

The fifth discovery: I believe God called David a man after His own heart because he knew how to confess and repent. We need to understand that, although David was a true worshipper, he was still a fallible human being of flesh and blood. Like any of us, he had his strengths and weaknesses.

My friend, there comes a time in our lives when, perhaps as a result of fame or fortune, we reach a place of complacency. We do not fast and pray as we should. We neglect our spiritual duties and responsibilities toward God, and we begin to settle into a condition of carelessness and indifference toward our Master. When this happens, we very soon find ourselves in trouble. I do believe that, at times like these, the Holy Spirit brings conviction to our spirit.

We know that we are heading downward and away from God. We then have a choice. We can turn around and repent; or we can ignore the Holy Spirit's warning and continue on our path to destruction. David reached this point of ease and complacency one day when he decided to take a walk on the rooftop of his house. Then he saw his neighbour's wife taking a bath in her home, and he desired to have her for himself.

I do believe with my whole heart that, when this idea came forth in his mind, the precious Holy Spirit was present to convict him of the terrible impending sin of adultery. David had a chance to respond to the Spirit's conviction and let go of this destructive idea. But, instead of yielding to the Spirit's call, he decided to follow through on the plan devised by the evil one. He was heading downward very fast!

Once again, my friend, the rest is history. He took Bathsheba, the wife of his army officer Uriah, for himself and committed adultery with her. One evil act soon led to another. From adultery, he progressed to murder, when he had Uriah killed in battle so he could have Bathsheba as his own wife. Bathsheba fell pregnant, and God decided to take the child. David's spiritual life was deteriorating very fast. But, just after he committed adultery with Bathsheba, God sent the Prophet Nathan to him with a very strong message.

God's message was one of termination. David was going to die because of this terrible sin. God was very serious about this evil sin. There was going to be no easy way out of this difficult problem for David. But once again, because David was a true worshipper and a man after God's own heart, he knew what to do at a time like this.

After Nathan had delivered his death sentence, David immediately fell to his knees and confessed his sin, and with remorse he turned to God in repentance. We can read the full text of his confession in *Psalm 51*, where he earnestly cried out to God for mercy and forgiveness. His honest, humble confession moved the heart of God. God forgave his sin and instructed Nathan to tell David, "The LORD... hath put away thy sin; thou shalt not die" (*2 Samuel 12:13*).

The Word of God declares in *1 John 1:9*, "If we confess our sins, he is faithful and just to forgive us our sins, and to cleanse us from all unrighteousness." We serve a God of mercy and forgiveness. All He expects of us is that we be willing to confess our sins and repent of our evil ways, and He will forgive us and give us another chance.

My friend, I do believe that God qualified David as a man after His own heart because, as a true worshipper, David knew how to confess and repent.

David Understood God's Priorities for Success

My sixth discovery: I believe God validated David as a man after His own heart because he understood God's priorities for success. At the apex of his life, when he was king over Israel, he faltered. He fell into sin with another man's wife and committed adultery and murder. God dealt seriously with him regarding those terrible transgressions.

He would not be a holy and righteous God if He had allowed David to get away with a simple slap on the wrist. Even though David was king over Israel, he had to suffer the consequences of his sinful actions. But you see, my friend, when you falter and fall by the wayside, God never gives up on you. Even when we give up on ourselves, God never gives up on us. He truly is a gracious and compassionate God whose mercies endure forever.

David knew this and, therefore, in his prayer of confession and repentance, he prayed for something very significant. In *Psalm 51*, he made the following supplication to God. Zeroing in on God's priority for a blessed and successful life, he pleaded, "Create in me a clean heart, O God; and renew a right spirit within me" (*Psalm 51:10*).

Two very important priorities for success. One, a clean heart. Two, a right spirit. In fact, the one complements the other. You cannot have the one without the other.

For anyone hoping to live a truly successful life, including a successful and blessed spiritual life, these two priorities are obligatory and compulsory. A clean heart speaks of honesty and truth in our daily lives. A right spirit speaks of a life of righteousness, obedience and submission to God. Living right and doing what is pleasing to God should at all times be our duty and our desire.

In the next verse, David touched on two more priorities for success. His plea to God was: "**Cast me not away from Thy presence; and take not Thy Holy Spirit from me**" (*Psalm 51:11*). In fact, these are the two most important components of a successful spiritual life: God's presence and His Holy Spirit.

Friend, to be in the presence of Almighty God is the best and safest place to be. It does not matter where you are. Country, city, town, or any other earthly location does not matter. Whether one is in church, at home, in the forest or in the open field, or anywhere on the face of the earth. You can experience the presence of Almighty God right there.

David knew what he was asking when he presented his request to God because, for most of his life as a young man, he constantly experienced God's holy presence wherever he was. To him, God's presence was as important as breathing and being alive. Life for him without God's presence would simply become a meaningless existence.

David desperately needed God to forgive him and not evict him from His holy presence. He understood perfectly well the importance of spending time in the presence of God.

His request was based on first-hand experience over many years as a Servant of God. For the servant of God to exist and maintain adequate spiritual growth, expansion and inspiration, it is imperative to spend much time in God's holy presence.

David then further expanded his request to God, asking Him not to take His Holy Spirit away from him. He fully understood the severe implications of God withdrawing His Holy Spirit from one's life. Earlier in this chapter, we referred to *1 Samuel 16:14*, which informed us that the Spirit of the Lord departed from Saul and an evil spirit troubled him. David was a first-hand witness of that terrible time, when an evil spirit ruled King Saul's life, and on several occasions David had to escape for his life.

Now he was facing that same possibility and reality. What would he do without the Spirit of God in his life? What terrible evil forces were lurking around, waiting to move in? He certainly would not survive the future without the Spirit of God to lead, guide and teach him like in past years.

David understood the importance of these priorities for a successful spiritual life, and he needed to have them in his future. He needed the presence of God and he needed the precious Holy Spirit of God. This brings us to priority number five. David pleaded with God, "Restore unto me the joy of Thy salvation; and uphold me with Thy free spirit" (*Psalm 51:12*).

Joy, real joy, is imperative in the life of the believer. *Nehemiah 8:10* says, "The joy of the LORD is your strength."

The terrible sins David committed had totally robbed him of the joy he once had in the Lord. Each time we sin wilfully, a part of the joy of God's salvation diminishes in our lives.

It is this joy of the Lord, of His salvation, that keeps us going from day to day, through the trials and tribulations of life. Satan is out to rob us of our joy—the very thing which makes life worth living and which energizes us to victory.

Romans 14:17b tells us that the kingdom of God is "righteousness, and peace, and joy in the Holy Ghost". This joy in the Holy Spirit, this joy of the Lord and of His salvation, is an integral part of being a child of God. It is the anthem of freedom and liberty for the child of God. It is our passport to victory in life's daily struggles. Once we have been robbed of this exhilarating and precious joy, we become weak and vulnerable to the attacks of the enemy, and he will have a field day with us.

Real joy, genuine joy in the Holy Spirit, is contagious to everyone around us. It lifts you up and uplifts those around you. It empowers you to face life's challenges without any fear or apprehension. It lifts you up to greater heights and motivates you to attempt greater exploits than before.

You feel like a champion; you feel you can conquer each and every foe. This was what enabled David to face the giant Goliath. He did not have any deadly weapon in his hand. What he had was the joy of the Lord uplifting him and boosting his faith. You and I know what happened to Goliath, the lion and the bear. They were destroyed by a young boy who lived in the joy of his Lord.

146

Next, David referred to the sacrifices acceptable to God:

For Thou desirest not sacrifice; else would I give it: Thou delightest not in burnt offering. The sacrifices of God are **a broken spirit**: **a broken and a contrite heart**, O God, **Thou wilt not despise**.

Psalm 51:16-17

This is another of God's priorities pertaining to confession and repentance. David would have offered a burnt offering for his sins if God had desired it. But, since a burnt offering would not be acceptable to Him, David offered what would please God instead: a *broken* spirit and a *broken* and contrite heart. Please note, if you will: the word "broken" is mentioned twice in *Psalm 51:16-17*.

God expects from us a broken spirit and a broken and contrite heart. No true confession or repentance can be regarded as genuine from God's vantage point, if it is not accompanied by tears, remorse and brokenness. For God to renew His Spirit within David, his human spirit had to be broken first of all. Similarly with me: only when my spirit, priorities and will are broken and destroyed can God's Spirit come into my life to bring restoration, renewal and revival.

Friends, I do believe that God was impressed with David because he fully understood, confessed and practised all of God's priorities for a successful spiritual life: a clean heart and a right spirit; God's presence and His Holy Spirit; the joy of the Lord and of His salvation; and the sacrifices of a broken spirit, and a broken and contrite heart. All these qualified David to be called a man after God's heart.

147

David Knew How to Cast Himself upon the Mercy of God

My seventh discovery: David knew how to submit to the Almighty and cast himself upon God's mercy. This incident is recorded in *2 Samuel 24*. David sinned because he decided to count God's people, against the warning of Joab, his general. He then had to face God's judgment and wrath.

One may ask, what is wrong with simply counting people? Why would God make such a big deal out of this? Well, my friend, I think God simply wanted David to understand and accept the fact that these were His people and not David's. Even though David had been anointed king over Israel, God was overall still in charge of His people. God was practically letting David know that it was His business alone to know how many of His people there were.

So God simply forbid David from counting His people. After he had the census conducted, David was sorry. He confessed his sin to God and begged Him for mercy. Then the Prophet Gath came to him with God's answer. God was giving David a choice of one of three punishments to be meted out to him and the people. David had disobeyed God's clear injunction against the census, and now the people had to bear the consequences of his sin.

Three sets of judgment were laid out before David

One: seven years of famine. Two: three months into the hands of his enemies. Three: three days of pestilence in the land. David had to decide which one of these three penalties should be implemented.

Then David made the following astounding statement to the Prophet Gath:

I am in a great strait [*in deep trouble*]; **let us fall now into the hand of the LORD; for His mercies are great: and let me not fall into the hand of man**.

2 Samuel 24:14

David chose the third option. He said he would rather fall into God's hand than into the hands of his enemies, because God's mercies were great. I believe this is another reason why David qualified to be called a man after God's own heart—because he knew how to cast himself on the mercy of Almighty God. Once again, you and I can learn much from David's beautiful example of absolute trust in God's mercy.

It does not matter how badly we have sinned, how terrible the deed we may have committed. God is waiting for us to turn to Him in confession and repentance. He will forgive us and cleanse us of all unrighteousness. In fact, the Word of God teaches that, after our confession and repentance, He will remember our sin no more.

Seems that God develops memory loss when it comes to confessed sin! He forgets the sins we have confessed and never thinks about them ever again! Isn't He a great and marvellous God? My friend, would you at this juncture like to join me in a prayer of confession and repentance? Let us pray the prayer on the following page.

Dear God and Heavenly Father, thank you for the wonderful example demonstrated to us by David, a man after your own heart. I want to ask for your forgiveness of the sins I have committed against my neighbours, friends and enemies. Lord, you know them by name.

I am sorry for all the sins and wrongs done against my neighbours over the past years. Please forgive me and cleanse me of all unrighteousness through the precious blood of your dear Son, Jesus Christ.

I now accept your forgiveness, and I thank you for making me totally clean. This I ask in the marvellous name of Jesus Christ.

Amen.

CHAPTER ELEVEN

Can these Bones Live?

The promise and possibility of genuine revival

L et us look now at Ezekiel chapter 37, as we consider the promise and possibility of genuine revival in our time. As previously mentioned, I regard the Prophet Ezekiel as the prophet of revival. He was the one prophet whom God brought down to the valley of dry bones, a place of death, devastation and total desolation, and there He challenged him to speak life into a situation of utter hopelessness.

It seemed that God had very special dealings with this man, and He had a significant task set aside for him. He was to be the one God would use to demonstrate the real meaning of revival from God's divine perspective. The prophet was very specific in his description of what happened in the valley of dry bones. First of all, he explained how God brought him to this desolate place:

> The hand of the LORD was upon me, and carried me out in the Spirit of the LORD, and set me down in the midst of the valley which was full of bones.
>
> *Ezekiel 37:1*

Then God had him walk through the valley, crisscrossing its length and breadth, so that he could ascertain the condition of the bones up close. God required an on-location, in-depth analysis of the true condition of those bones.

After a careful inspection, the prophet reported that "there were very many in the open valley; and, lo, they were very dry!" (*Ezekiel 37:2*) If they were very dry, it is clear that they must have been in the valley for a long time. Those bones used to belong in the living bodies of real people. But, when Ezekiel saw them, they were simply dry bones lying about, out there in the hot midday sun. There used to be life in them, but not anymore; they were just lifeless, dry bones.

Friends, as I look at the Church today, in comparison to the New Testament Church, it would seem we are seeing a similar situation in our midst. The Church worldwide is huge and massive. Internationally, church membership has probably run into billions by now. The Church, the Body of Christ, is represented in most of the nations around the world, even in atheistic countries where the Gospel of Jesus Christ is prohibited. God's Church is like a huge sleeping giant. Huge and powerful, but sleeping and very silent.

The Church today looks nothing like the New Testament Church that was created, planted and established by God on the day of Pentecost. The fervent and vibrant enthusiasm with which the early Christians proclaimed God's life-giving message of salvation to a lost world is no longer evident or relevant today—whether in our proclamation, presentation or demonstration of this same message. We are like a sea of very dry bones, asleep down in the midst of a vast valley of unbelief, despondency and lethargy. What used to be a mighty army of life-giving vessels of hope to a dying world now looks like something of absolutely no consequence.

The world had respect for the New Testament Church, even though they persecuted its members. Today, the world has no respect for the Church. People look at the Church with scepticism and scorn because it is no longer the Church as God intended it to be.

The early Christians' enthusiasm and excitement about Jesus Christ, who He is and what He is able to do for us, seem to have dwindled and disappeared from our midst. Now we simply go through the motions in our worship services, without the presence of God and the genuine anointing of the Holy Spirit. No longer do we approach God's house with great expectations of a divine encounter with Almighty God.

Much of what we try to do for God is ineffective because it is fashioned according to our own agendas. Things are pretty much dead, dry and dreary in most churches. The precious Holy Spirit is patiently waiting outside of our impressive and marvellous sanctuaries and crystal cathedrals, waiting to be invited into His rightful place.

God the Holy Spirit is not able to fulfil His divine assignment in our midst because He has been very diplomatically evicted from our sanctuaries. We are running His programme and doing the tasks assigned to Him by Almighty God.

Precious souls are not being saved and added to the Kingdom of God. The sick, the maimed, the despondent, the rejected and troubled souls are not being ministered to. Marriages and families in our churches are disintegrating right before our eyes.

The ministry of the Church of Jesus Christ in general seems to have become insignificant and ineffective. Psychologists and psychiatrists are now trying to deal with spiritual issues in our communities—issues which have long been assigned to God's Church and actually belong in the domain of Spirit-filled Servants of God. Yes, my friend, it seems the present condition of the Church in our day matches Ezekiel's vision of the valley of dry bones.

Then came God's question: "Son of man, can these bones live?" God was waiting on Ezekiel's answer.

And he answered the Lord, "O Lord GOD, Thou knowest" (*Ezekiel 37:3*). In other words, Ezekiel was placing the "ball" back in God's court. He was saying that only God was able to address this impossible condition. But then God placed the ball right back in the prophet's court.

He said to Ezekiel, "Prophesy upon these bones..." God had anointed and empowered him as His Prophet to deal adequately with the situation. Ezekiel had the ability to speak to this impossible situation and change the status quo. The anointing resting upon his life was the key to revolutionizing and changing the scene of death to one of brand new life!

God instructed Ezekiel to prophesy to the multitude of dry bones. He was to cry out and proclaim unto them, "O ye dry bones, hear the word of the LORD!" (*Ezekiel 37:4*) The key for revival today, my friend, is for us to "hear the Word of the Lord!" Hallelujah!

God was about to perform a miracle right in front of Ezekiel's eyes, should he be obedient to prophesy the word of the Lord. If he would be willing to do his part, God would do the rest. Even today, God's miracle-working power is resident in His holy Word. When we speak God's Word, God will back it up every time, with signs following.

We need to hear the pure, unadulterated Word of God preached without prejudice, preference or compromise. When we study *Ezekiel 37:5-6*, we notice how, step by step, God instructed the prophet to speak life into those dry bones. Ezekiel was to conclude his prophecy with the words, "And ye shall live; and ye shall know that I am the LORD!"

Ezekiel reported that, when he started prophesying, "there was a noise, and behold a shaking, and the bones came together, bone to his bone." Then sinews, flesh and skin came forth to cover the bones, but there was no breath in them (*Ezekiel 37:7-8*). Ezekiel was next instructed to prophesy life-giving Spirit into the dead bodies.

In obedience to God's command, Ezekiel prophesied life into the dead bodies:

> So I prophesied as He commanded me, and the breath came into them, and they lived, and stood up upon their feet, an exceeding great army!
>
> *Ezekiel 37:10*

As the word of prophesy went forth from the mouth of God's prophet, life came forth. An exceedingly great army stood to their feet, ready for action. The life-giving Word of God is what God's servants need to prophesy in our day!

We need God's servants to speak up and speak out the life-giving Word, which is able to renew, transform and revive the Church and restore us to our original glorious state. The precious Holy Spirit, endowed with significant ministries and gifts available to the church, should be allowed to return to His rightful place in the sanctuary. The man servants and maid servants of Almighty God should rise boldly to their feet in proclamation of the Word of God.

The anointing, presence and glory of Almighty God should permeate and saturate the house of God. True Holy Spirit revival will usher in a brand new type of Christian who is willing to discard all unholy things in his or her life, home and community. A new wave of holiness will sweep over our churches, our cities and our nations, and respect for God's Church and God's people will once again become evident.

As this mighty army of God, revived from the ashes of apostasy, abomination and indifference, rises to its feet in holy worship, praise and adoration, I believe this world will be shaken by God's power like never before. World leaders will once again respect the Church and call upon us to take the lead in the restoration process. The Church will once again be the head and not the tail.

Above and not beneath. The leader and not the follower. Once again, we will be able to truly say to the world, "Thus says the Lord God Almighty!" No longer will there be any compromise. No longer will we follow the so-called leaders in our communities who have no respect for the holy things of God. We will be the leaders. We will speak the Word, and God will confirm the Word with signs following.

The church will act and move with New Testament boldness and Holy Spirit power, even in the face of persecution and prosecution. God's mighty army will stand firm on the immovable Rock of Ages, on the rock of His divine Word, and will execute His divine commands with total commitment, dedication and resolve. God will visit His Church with power and glory and, through His Church, He will visit the nations of the world with a demonstration of His power and glory, the like of which we have never witnessed before. Hallelujah! Bless the glorious name of Jesus!

So, my friend, in answer to the question posed to our modern-day Ezekiels—"Can these bones live?"—we can reply with confidence, boldness and exuberance, "Oh yes, these dead and very dry bones can surely live again!" Not only can they live again, but they will be able to bring about glorious renewal and genuine revival around the world.

On the day of Pentecost, the Apostle Peter, quoting from the Prophet Joel, declared God's promise to pour out His Spirit upon all flesh in the last days (*Acts 2:16-18*). Life-giving words will go forth and bring new life into the Church and into our communities.

I do believe that we have already entered those last days referred to by the prophet. This is the time for God's visitation! The conditions in the world and in the Church are such that a divine visitation by Almighty God has become imperative. Almighty God is the only hope and the only answer to our problems!

Friends, I believe God is about to confirm the promise of revival in our day. He is about to pour out His Spirit upon all flesh. Church, get ready! It's about to happen!

Now, my friend, please join me in this short prayer:

Heavenly Father, I ask you for a divine visitation and encounter in my life, in my family, in our church, in our community, in our country, and throughout the world.

Come Holy Spirit, move in and take your rightful place in our midst. Take over! Reign, Jesus, reign! Be Lord! Change us, renew us, and revive us! In Jesus' precious Name, Amen.

CHAPTER TWELVE

Good for One Thing or Good for Nothing

Fulfilling the purpose for which we were created

Ezekiel chapter 15 starts off with God comparing His people to the wood of the vine. He posed a question: "how is the wood of the grapevine (Israel) better than any wood... among the trees of the forest?" (*Ezekiel 15:2, AMP*) Can the wood of the vine be used for any commercial or domestic purpose? (*Ezekiel 15:3-5*) Is there any special use for it? When it stands there planted in the vineyard, is it of any good use except to produce bunches of grapes hanging from its branches?

Then God answered His own question, and what He said was very significant. The wood of the vine is actually good for only one thing. To stand there, planted in the soil of the earth, bearing the fruit it was designed to produce. That's it. It is good for only one thing. If it fulfils this purpose, then it has value. If not, it is good for nothing except to be burnt in the fire. Wow! What a lesson! Good for only one thing, or good for nothing!

For all of us, this lesson should be very important. We should take heed of the consequences of not fulfilling the purpose for which we have been created. I hope this lesson will motivate all of us to be what God has created us to be.

As I mentioned in the preceding chapters, we have been created by God for the specific purpose of worshipping Him and Him only. We have been created to worship Him in spirit and in truth. That was God's purpose in creating us. Created for this one single purpose. To worship Him only.

We have been created as God's Creatures of Worship. That was God's prime objective when He made us. Throughout history and over many centuries, He has been trying to bring us to the point where we will accept and embrace His purpose for us. But, thus far, God's message has not successfully filtered through to all of us. Many of us are still worshipping other things, to the exclusion of the God of all creation. In other words, we are still busy practising idol worship, which is an abomination to God.

My friend, God is saying we should be worshipping only Him. That is our purpose. That is God's will. We should be good at worshipping only God. God expects us to be good at worshipping Him in spirit and in truth! We should excel in this awesome assignment of genuine worship to the true and living God. True worship of Almighty God alone should be our daily lifestyle. We should be good in this one thing. If not, then we are good for nothing; we are only good for the fire.

You see, dearly beloved, God is serious about worship! He demands our total allegiance and loyalty. Nothing less will do. He is a jealous God! With Him there can be no half-hearted attempts. No fifty-fifty worship. We either do it properly and appropriately, or we do not do it at all.

God told the church in Laodicea, "because thou art lukewarm, and neither cold nor hot, I will spew thee out of my mouth" (*Revelation 3:16*). God is not impressed by lukewarm, half-hearted attempts at worship. Worship is not something we can play with, doing it just when we feel like it. It should be a lifestyle. Worship should be genuine. So if we are not going to be good at true worship, then God says we are good for nothing. Either good for the one thing, true worship, or good for nothing but the flames of the fire.

Love Must Motivate Us to Worship God

Love, my friend, is the motivator for our being here today. Because this is who Almighty God is, love motivated Him to create the universe and everything we see around us. Love was what motivated our Lord Jesus to come to this sinful world to be our Saviour and Redeemer. He said, regarding His love for us: "Greater love hath no man than this, that a man lay down his life for his friends" (*John 15:13*).

Indeed, as the Apostle John has declared, the greatest love ever revealed is God's love for us:

> For God so loved the world, that He gave His only begotten Son, that whosoever believeth in Him should not perish, but have everlasting life.
>
> *John 3:16*

True love was what motivated God to reach out to us, touch us, and change our lives through our Lord Jesus.

Love is the key theme throughout the Old and New Testaments. It runs like a golden thread right through the Bible. God has unequivocally proven His unconditional love for us, and He requires you and me to reciprocate by loving Him back. We should love the Lord our God with everything we are and have, to the exclusion of all other gods. God made this very clear in His first commandment (*Exodus 20:3*).

Jesus one day asked Peter a very simple but significant question. He asked him three times in succession: "Do you love me?" (*John 21:15-17*) Peter was very grieved by Jesus' question.

But, my friend, Jesus knew very well why He was posing this question—because, before Christ was crucified, Peter had denied that he ever knew Him. This was the same man who had told Jesus before His crucifixion that he was willing to follow Him all the way and even die for Him. Then came the test of his allegiance to his Master, and he failed it.

My friend, even though Peter dismally failed the test, God never gave up on him. In fact, he was already forgiven when in tears he turned and looked at Jesus after the cock crowed three times. The look that Jesus gave him was full of pity, love and forgiveness. This failure of a man was later to become God's choice instrument, mightily used by Him on the day of Pentecost. This same failure would become instrumental in the establishment of the Christian Church around the world.

What if God should pose that very same question to us today? Do you, my friend, love God? Do you really love Him? Do you love our Saviour Jesus Christ? Do you really love Him? Do you love the Holy Spirit? Do you really love Him?

If the answer is yes, then the next question presents an even greater challenge. How much do you love Him? How much do you love your God? Enough to go all the way with Him? Enough to sacrifice and lose all in order to please Him, in the way that the Apostle Paul did? Paul declared:

> I count all things but loss for the Excellency of the knowledge of Christ Jesus my Lord: for whom I have suffered the loss of all things, and do count them but dung, that I may win Christ.
>
> *Philippians 3:8*

Wow! What a statement! Willing to lose everything in order to please and worship Jesus Christ! Do we love God in this uncompromising manner? Is He really and truly Number One in our lives? Is He really *Numero Uno*? Jesus declared in *John 14:15*, "If ye love me, keep my commandments." In other words: "If you love me, do my Father's will. Do what pleases my heavenly Father. Do what pleases me." What pleases God is that we love Him unconditionally, and serve and worship Him only, without any compromise.

Friend, we cannot truly worship God in spirit and in truth if we do not love Him unconditionally. Our love for our Lord must motivate us to surrender our all to Him and totally submit to His divine will. Anything less will not do.

Anything less will not take us to the higher level of anointing, blessing, breakthrough, and victorious life available to true worshippers. Love must be the motivator. We must love the Lord with all that is within us, and we must love our neighbour as ourselves.

Even if it is difficult to get along with some people in our midst, God expects us to love them. This is possibly the hardest thing to do, to love those who hate us or are difficult to get along with. Love must be our motivator. The path to victory for God's people runs through the wonderful garden of real, genuine love. If we truly have the love of God in our hearts, then loving others should not be impossible.

True Worship 24/7

What is true worship 24/7? How does one worship God 24 hours a day, seven days a week? What is a 24/7 worship lifestyle? Well, my friend, it actually is very easy and simple. God has provided us with a very plain and simple Gospel. The message of salvation is very simple. We have the whole message of salvation in a nutshell in *John 3:16*. It is so easy and simple. Anyone can read it—or we can have it read to us—and understand its contents.

The same goes for true worship 24/7. If we truly are God's Creatures of Worship, we ought to be engaged in 24/7 worship, just like the Seraphim are worshipping before God's holy throne at this very moment. They are engaged in continuous true worship 24/7.

How then do we, as God's earthly Seraphim, practise this exact same mode of worship? Friend, we worship Him in everything we do. Everything we say. Everywhere we go. Everything we write. In each and every communication we engage in. We worship Him when we get up in the morning, in the manner we say "Good morning" to our spouse and kids, to our parents and our other family members.

We worship Him when we take a bath or shower, get dressed, eat breakfast, get into our automobile and drive to work or drive the kids to school. We worship God in the manner we do our job at the office or in the way we do our daily chores at home, in the kitchen and throughout our homes. We worship God in the manner we act and interact with others in the store, in the mall, on the bus or on the train. We worship God with each and every move we make in our 24-hour day.

We worship Him with our mind, as we utilize this marvellous organ He gave called the brain. We worship Him with the tongue in our mouth, when we speak to one another or sing praises to Him with the vocal cords He has given us. We can thus worship our Lord anytime, anywhere, and in any manner. No fixed place or timeslot can set limits to our worship. My soul, mind, body and spirit will be totally in sync with the Holy Spirit at all times, since I have now become a 24/7 true worshipper.

The Apostle Paul, writing to the church in Philippi, exhorted them to become 24/7 true worshippers by having their mind, soul, spirit and body in sync with the Holy Spirit.

This is what he wrote in his letter to them:

> Finally, brethren, whatsoever things are true, whatsoever things are honest, whatsoever things are just, whatsoever things are pure, whatsoever things are lovely, whatsoever things are of good report; if there be any virtue, and if there be any praise, think on these things.
>
> *Philippians 4:8*

Dear friends, as we strive to have the mind of Christ (*Philippians 2:5; 1 Corinthians 2:16*) and to become more like Him—taking Him as our example—we will be transformed. We will start to move to a higher level of communication with Him. It will then be our desire and top priority to fill our minds with those things which Paul talked about: all that is true, honest, just, pure, lovely and righteous (of good report); all that edifies and empowers us to become genuine Christians and thus true worshippers of God.

True 24/7 worship will become our daily lifestyle when we successfully acquire and practise the virtues of truth, honesty, justice, purity, loveliness, righteousness (good report), and all that is godly and praiseworthy. The Prophet Isaiah also confirmed this important issue of the sanctification of our minds when he declared, "Thou wilt keep him in perfect peace, whose mind is stayed on Thee: because he trusteth in Thee" (*Isaiah 26:3*).

The Apostle Paul also exhorts us: "Whether therefore ye eat, or drink, or whatsoever ye do, do all to the glory of God" (*1 Corinthians 10:31*). Well, my friend, that is 24/7 worship.

Please note the words: "whatsoever ye do". To my understanding, this means that everything we do daily ought to be directed at the God whom we serve and worship. In this manner, we will be practising continuous 24/7 true worship.

In closing, would you please just imagine the following scenario with me? What if God the Holy Spirit, from this day forward, could succeed in establishing this 24/7 lifestyle of true worship desired by Almighty God in each of our lives? What if we, as humans in general and as God's people in particular, can hook into this awesome vision of being truly God's earthly Creatures of Worship, operating in this glorious 24/7 true worship lifestyle?

What if we as God's Church are able, with the inspiration and empowerment of the Holy Spirit, to engage in continuous 24/7 worship of Almighty God in everything we do and say? My, oh my! My friend, needless to say, our lives, our homes, our marriages, our families, our communities, our towns and cities, our countries, and eventually the whole world will become an absolute paradise!

May I dare to say I believe with all my heart that this is exactly what God has intended for us? This is exactly what Almighty God has purposed for us, as His Creatures of Worship here on earth. Then there will certainly be "peace among men", as was proclaimed by the host of angels on the night of our Lord's birth (*Luke 2:14*). There will be peace, harmony and understanding in our homes and everywhere else on earth. God our Creator will be the focus of all of our worship, our activities, and our total existence. Hallelujah!

I am sure we all desire to see this come to pass. Well, my friend, you and I can start working on this marvellous vision today, right here, right now. One by one, we can establish God's divine Kingdom among us right here, right now, by truly becoming God's earthly Creatures of Worship. I believe with all my heart that God desires His people to be true worshippers, ready and willing to worship Him in spirit and in truth 24/7. I marvel at the possibilities, miracles and breakthroughs available to us, when we as true worshippers succeed in tapping into God's source of supernatural power.

Conclusion

My dear friend, I really trust that God's Word has touched your heart in the same manner He has touched and changed mine. Not only has He touched my heart, God has truly transformed, renewed and revived my Christian life through the truths He revealed to me regarding true worship—truths which I have shared in this book.

I have personally recommitted and rededicated my life, my ministry, and my future to JESUS CHRIST, MY LORD, MY MASTER AND MY KING. I have confessed my faults, my sins, and my iniquities before Him, and He has forgiven me. Hallelujah! I am a brand new man, a brand new servant of the Most High God. I feel great. I feel good. I am ready and willing to be used by God.

I am a child of the King of kings and the Lord of lords, and I am a co-heir of the Kingdom with my Lord Jesus Christ. Yes, I am a Creature of Worship, created by Almighty God to worship Him alone, in spirit and in truth. I am a true worshipper of the Most High God! I have decided to be excellent at the one thing for which I have been created, which is to worship Him only! Hallelujah! Praise the name of Jesus Christ!

My friend, would you like to join me? Do you want to be a true worshipper of Almighty God, worshipping Him in spirit and in truth? If you are certain and serious, please join me now for this final prayer of dedication and consecration.

Heavenly Father, KING of all kings and LORD of all lords, I bow before your holy throne in humble submission. On this day, I dedicate and consecrate my life to you as a true worshipper.

Lord, I acknowledge that I have made mistakes in the past. I thought I was worshipping you, but I have discovered that I fall hopelessly short of your mark. Lord, I want to worship you in spirit and in truth, 24 hours a day, 7 days a week.

Help me from this day forward to make you the number one priority in my life. I surrender my all to you. I am yours, to serve and to worship you. I place all my problems and difficulties in your capable hands, knowing you will take care of me and my family. Use me, Lord, for your divine glory. In the precious name of our Lord and Saviour Jesus Christ. Amen.

Please declare with me once again:

"I am God's Creature of Worship, created by Almighty God to worship Him alone, in spirit and in truth, now and forever. Amen."

Now let us give praise, honour and glory to our Almighty God, who alone is worthy to be worshipped in Spirit and in Truth 24/7!

About the Author

Bishop Dr Peter L. Coetzee was born and raised in Cape Town, South Africa. He is the Founder and President of The Church of New Hope International. He has also established several other local and national ministries and ministered internationally.

Dr Coetzee's 51 years of international ministry have taken him to several African and European countries, as well as to the USA, where he and his wife ministered nationally for six years, and where he was also featured on several local religious radio and television channels. They later returned to Cape Town, South Africa, where Dr Coetzee now ministers regularly as a conference speaker, seminar presenter, workshop leader, author, singer, songwriter, and music composer and arranger. His messages and music are featured regularly on Christian radio stations in South Africa.

Coinciding with the writing and first publication of his book, *Creature of Worship*, he established "The Creature of Worship Network Ministry". More information about this ministry may be found on the following page.

Dr Coetzee holds Bachelor's, Master's and Doctor's degrees in Theology and Divinity. Sidonia Coetzee, his wife of more than 46 years, has been his faithful and strong supporter and companion in his ministry. Their only daughter, Lavinia Celaire, currently resides in Toronto, Canada, with her husband Rich and their two daughters Evangeline and Gabrielle.

Contact: P.O. Box 449, Bellville 7535 South Africa
Email: plcoetz44@yahoo.com

About Creature of Worship Network Ministry

Creature of Worship Network Ministry was founded in 2006 with the objective of establishing a global network of true worshippers within the Body of Christ internationally. This is not a church, nor is it a denomination or organization; we are simply a network of believers who desire to join hands, hearts and spirits as true worshippers in holy worship of our precious Lord and Saviour Jesus Christ. We are hoping to mobilize believers residing in every city and town all around the world to become God's agents of true worship in their areas of influence.

We believe this could enhance and further the cause of worship amongst believers in churches everywhere, ignite fires of revival within the Body of Christ worldwide, and lead to renewal in God's Church. Once we begin to understand the message of true worship, the potential for revival in our time will indeed become a glorious reality.

For further information, please visit our website:
www.creatureofworship.faithweb.com

Or write to the author:
Email address: plcoetz44@yahoo.com

Other Products
A number of CDs recorded by the Author and also his Instrumental CDs are available on our website.

www.ingramcontent.com/pod-product-compliance
Lightning Source LLC
LaVergne TN
LVHW051629080426
835511LV00016B/2263